AF654270

INVISIBLE FORGOTTEN SUFFERERS

The Plight of Widows Around the World

INVISIBLE FORGOTTEN SUFFERERS

The Plight of Widows Around the World

VIJAY DUTT

Research by

RISTO F. HARMA

Commissioned by

International Widows Day

June 23

THE LOOMBA FOUNDATION

Caring for Widows around the World

KONARK PUBLISHERS PVT LTD

KONARK PUBLISHERS PVT LTD
206, First Floor, Peacock Lane,
Shahpur Jat, New Delhi-110049
e-mail: konarkpublishers@hotmail.com

Distribution (Worldwide)
THE LOOMBA FOUNDATION
Loomba House
622, Western Avenue,
London W3 0TF
Tel: 020 8896 9922
Email: mail@theloombafoundation.org
www.theloombafoundation.org

Copyright © The Loomba Foundation, 2010

ISBN 81-220-0785-6

All rights reserved. No part of this book may be reproduced or utilized in any form or by any means, electronic or mechanical, including photocopying, recording, or by any information storage and retrieval system, without prior permission in writing from the publishers.

Typeset by The Laser Printers, New Delhi, and printed at
ASK Advertising Aids Pvt Ltd., New Delhi.

Saikat Majumdar

FOREWORD

If there was ever any justification needed for the work of the Loomba Foundation of which I have been President for a decade, it can be found within the pages of this book.

Here you will find unimaginable horrors inflicted on impoverished widows and their children in the Third World following the already tragic loss of their husbands and fathers.

As a life-long active human rights campaigner, I see my role with the Foundation as being an extension of this, reaching out a helping hand to one of the most deprived groups of people on the global stage today.

Today, as an accredited UN NGO, we are active in nine countries in South Asia and Africa and will continue to expand to meet the global emergency.

In India, where our work started, we continue to educate over 3,000 children of impoverished widows across all the 29 States.

In South Africa, in partnership with Sir Richard Branson's Charity Virgin Unite, we helped establish a community-based project for 1,500 orphans of HIV victims.

In Sri Lanka, Bangladesh, Nepal, Kenya and Uganda—working alongside the Youth Business International, a Prince of Wales charity—we have launched entrepreneurial projects to help widows set up small businesses, so they can feed and educate their children.

In Rwanda, we have established a major programme to help genocide widows in association with Oxfam and the Mayor of Kigali.

In addition to our work on the ground, we continue to campaign internationally for the UN to recognise June 23 as the International Widows Day. Our objective is to focus the attention of the entire world on the severe deprivation faced by large numbers of widows and their children.

When you read this book, you will understand why...

Cherie Blair
President
The Loomba Foundation

ACKNOWLEDGEMENTS

The portrayal of the tragic state of widows across the world needed more than statistical data and graphs. It was necessary to understand their emotional trauma and the interplay of customs, rites, and social degradation and deprivation that inflict such brutality on them. The woman might have been a mother, a sister, and a respected elder, but once widowed, she loses all status, indeed relationships, and is stigmatised and ostracised.

I have attempted to narrate their plight in the following pages. But, more importantly, I have tried to put their woes in perspective so that people, international agencies, governments and philanthropists realise the inhuman treatment society metes out to widows, who along with their dependents and adult children, number almost one-sixth of the world's population. It is a human rights issue.

These objectives could not have been achieved without the Widows Research Report put together by researcher Risto F. Harma, based on a survey by the World Public Opinion and facilitated by the Royal Institute for International Affairs (Chatham House). The Report was commissioned by the Loomba Foundation. It is because of the remarkable research by Harma, which must have called for great reserves of perseverance and patience that I could write this book. In fact, it is he who gave me a sharper insight into the problems widows have endured for long in most developing countries.

I am also thankful to the reports prepared by several organisations in Africa and, of course, agencies of the United Nations. Risto's research for the Widows Research Report included consultation with internationally renowned researchers Professor Sylvia Chant of the London School of Economics, a specialist in international gender issues, and Professor Paul Spicker, a specialist in poverty and its measurement, at Robert Gordon University, Scotland, among others.

Most importantly, I owe my thanks to the Loomba Foundation for entrusting me with the responsibility of writing this book. Mr. Raj Loomba, CBE handed me the Research Report, simply asking me to write the "story" of the tragedy of widowhood, while bringing out the almost callous neglect of widows and their children the world over. The book will help the Loomba Foundation convince the United Nations that nearly 245 million widows across the globe have been deprived of their human rights.

I must also thank our Publisher Mr. K.P.R. Nair, who had had to produce the book in a very short time, and Mr. K.G. Sreenivas who edited the book and helped bring sharper focus in the book on the world of widows.

Vijay Dutt

CONTENTS

International Widows Day June 23

THE LOOMBA FOUNDATION
Caring for Widows around the World

INTRODUCTION

The word 'widow' was almost unknown and incomprehensible to me until my father died. I was just over 10 years old. It was agonising to see how my mother, who was until then a happy and contented housewife and a loving mother to us (four sons and three daughters), was, even in her traumatised state, made to take off her bangles, remove her *bindi* and wear white clothes. My father's passing had shut her out from the world, or so it seemed.

There was more to come. At my wedding, in the midst of the rituals, my mother was asked to leave. It was said that being a widow she would bring bad luck to me in my married life. That was the most agonising moment for me. I went through various emotions: pain, anguish, anger and a feeling of frustration. How could my mother who had brought me up with so much care and love be unlucky for me?

Fortunately for us, my father, who was a successful and affluent businessman, had left his family enough money. My mother spent it educating all of us at the best institutions and she sent me to America for higher studies. However, after the marriage of my three sisters there was little money left. There would be nothing that I could do if I returned home to Punjab. Instead I went to Great Britain where my elder brother had settled. It was the beginning of a long fight to find my feet.

I did everything, mopping floors, driving ice-cream vans and selling garments from temporary wayside stalls. My mother's blessings, I am sure, helped me. My business ventures succeeded and I was on my way to establishing a multi-national garments industry.

But I remained restless. Why was my mother made to change from a woman to a widow? Why was it believed that she would bring bad luck to me? It also struck me, 'what if my father was not prosperous and had left us no money?' My mother would not have been able to send us to college or give us nutritious food and good clothes to wear. The images and the state of poor widows and their children I had seen in my younger days all came rushing back to me. It was troubling. If I was a son of a poor widow, I would not have been living in London overseeing a major export company. I would have grown up, an illiterate man, possibly plying a rickshaw in some suburban town in Punjab.

I decided that I would try to help educate children of poor widows. Doing so would not only give hope to widows, but also ensure that their children might grow up with enough qualifications and opportunities to face a different future. Their children might not have to face poverty too.

It seemed natural that I should form a Trust in the name of my mother for funding the schooling of widows' children. The Shrimati Pushpa Wati Loomba Foundation was first set up in the UK and then launched in India in 1999 by the then Indian Prime Minister. Since I knew the plight of widows in India better, I made it my mission to educate, initially, 100 children of poor widows in each Indian state. I am happy to report that the mission was achieved in just a few years. Today the Foundation is educating over 3,000 children in the country.

During the course of meeting the children I saw the condition of their mothers. They looked as if they were resigned to their humiliations, utter penury and a daily struggle to survive. Hopelessness was writ large on their faces. So it was not enough to just help educate their children, they too needed help. They were the faceless living dead, forgotten by their families, society and the state. I decided to take up their cause, to help them become women again, to be equal members of society. This was only possible, however, if they could be empowered and given the confidence and the capability to earn their livelihood independently. The decision made, I expanded the objectives of the Foundation, but soon realised that I had set upon a long and arduous journey. There were age-old hurdles, superstitions and beliefs. In fact, the magnitude and the complexity of the whole issue of widows hit me when I started to travel to developing countries to personally understand the conditions of widows in different communities, the customs and traditions that seemed to swamp all laws and welfare measures of governments to help them.

I encountered another problem. It was, in fact, the biggest hurdle. There was an acute dearth of information about widows. The Trust then commissioned a research project to collect all possible information about widows across the world and to compile and compute all relevant statistics.

It was not an easy task. Hostile atmospheres, closed societies, difficult and inaccessible remote areas, war-torn countries and a few states which loathed parting with any information about their society. But I am proud to say that the Foundation now has, in the Widows Research Report, comprehensive information about widows the world over. It contains facts, hitherto unknown. Every facet and every factor affecting widowhood has been compiled. The Research Report 2010 covers 10 thematic areas and 45 individual topics and it is the first full and comprehensive compilation of the state of widows on a global scale.

The Report made me realise again how big and complex the issue of widows is. They number 245 million and if each has on average four children, the problem affects nearly a billion people worldwide. We are talking about one-sixth of humanity. This mass of humanity has been suffering and living in the most inhuman situations. Forgotten, anonymous and near outcasts!

The magnitude of the problem, however, did not deter the Foundation. We started our work and I am proud that in just a few years the Foundation has been able to help widows in various countries in Africa and the Indian sub-continent. Many have been 'empowered' through skill training and by setting up cooperatives where they learn, earn and find companionship amongst women in a similar situation. Through economic empowerment of poor widows they will also become empowered socially and politically. They will become an asset for a nation instead of being a burden.

The Foundation also conceived the strategy of creating awareness about the issues of widows and their sufferings. The campaign for awareness and for governments, companies and people to join our mission was launched by holding the International Widows Day on June 23 in London.

It caught on and now the International Widows Day is held every year in several countries, including at the United Nations in New York. On that day, apart from representatives of groups working for helping widows, ministers, officials, diplomats and corporate heads come together to help us achieve our goal to 'rescue' all widows in the world by empowering them. Information is gathered, reports of completed work are analysed, and more crucially, more people join our efforts to help widows.

Every International Widows Day, I am happy to say, creates more awareness among governments and people and more plans are formulated to help them further. This has put a smile back on the faces of thousands of widows in various developing countries.

The Loomba Foundation has made huge strides to highlight the plight of widows globally—particularly with the continued and invaluable support from our President Cherie Blair and our Trustee Lord Dholakia, who are the pillars of the Loomba Foundation. I must also thank Patrons, Trustees, Advisers, Corporate Heads and many individuals who have joined the Foundation in its endeavour to help widows. However, we have a long way to go.

Every International Widows Day events have been attended by senior politicians, diplomats and philanthropists, all of whom welcomed the Foundation's work and more importantly helped too. It was in no small way that their support of our work led to the Foundation being given official accreditation as a United Nations Non-Governmental Organisation (NGO).

Although the Foundation has achieved some success in what initially appeared to be 'Mission Impossible', the objective of salvaging all 245 million widows will never be achieved unless the governments, businesses and people across the world sincerely unite to tackle this huge and human issue.

The International Widows Day provides the opportunity to every international welfare agency, states, corporations and societies to highlight the issue on one day in every part of the world. This true coming together of nations and peoples on a particular day every year is only possible if the United Nations recognises June 23 and officially declares it as the UN International Widows Day.

It has admitted that widows are victims of 'Sins of Omission'. The time is now for the UN to address and tackle those sins of omission. The Loomba Foundation and many other organisations are ready and willing to put their resources to join in its efforts to help save and rehabilitate the 245 million widows and their dependants from being trampled upon by obscurantist beliefs, outdated systems and an inhuman mindset.

It's an issue of human rights. Widows are victims of all possible violations of human rights. And the UN is the only institution in the world that is a watchdog for outrages that deprive people of their human rights.

This book, commissioned by the Loomba Foundation, along with the Widows Research Report, details the plight of widows and their children in each and every society in the world. They present, in detail, the causes and the effects of widowhood and they enumerate the methods by which self-esteem and a more just future can be restored to these women and their children.

I hope that in this year, 2010, the United Nations will undertake the restoration of human rights to all the widows all over the globe. The beginning could be the official declaration of June 23 as the UN International Widows Day.

International Widows Day June 23
THE LOOMBA FOUNDATION
Caring for Widows around the World

Raj Loomba, CBE
Founder and Chairman Trustee
The Loomba Foundation

1

THE DEPRIVED ONE-SIXTH OF HUMANITY

They suffer deprivation, discrimination and humiliation

She was 12 when she was married. At 16 she was widowed. At 18, she was in the sex trade. Her woes began soon after her husband died.

She resigned herself to her fate of anonymity until her brother-in-law, her late husband's elder brother, raped her. He warned her that if she complained, he would say that she enticed him by stripping in front of him and she would be thrown out of her home. However, an even more catastrophic destiny was in store for her. One day the sister-in-law found her husband with the widow. She was thrown out.

This horrific story is of a child widow of a lower middle class family. However, even older widows of upper middle class families are also often forced to live wretched lives.

This abandonment is the culmination of her life, one that was built around her husband. She is ousted from the family, society and from the world she lived in and knew and abandoned to rebuild her life all over again. Her family does not want her and society couldn't care less. She is deprived of everything she had as a wife. The husband's death eclipsed her life. There is no emotional support, hope, nor future.

Suffering in isolation and obscurity, she shares the fate of millions of widows across the globe—245 million in 2010 according to The Loomba Foundation-sponsored Widows Research Report.

International agencies, women's organisations and governments have helped draft and legislate anti-discrimination laws and have initiated steps for poverty alleviation, but almost all such measures have bracketed widows with women in general. However, a widow is seldom treated as a woman in developing countries. The measures for helping women thus rarely benefit them. This has only helped perpetuate their abuse.

They lose not only their husbands but their protectors too. Ousted and ostracised, they are thrown out from families and communities. The result is that poverty alleviation or anti-discrimination programmes carried out by international or women's agencies rarely benefit widows.

A survey of the state of widows in developing countries highlights their distressing existence and the immediate need to rescue them from barbaric customs, out-dated religious beliefs and humiliating treatment.

According to tradition, Kenyan widows face eviction by in-laws who evoke the customary law to claim that they have no rights in their marital homes. Some widows are coerced into unions with a relative (of the deceased husband) who 'inherits' her as part of the husband's estate.

Apart from facing eviction by in-laws, they are reportedly also likely to be thrown out if they refuse to be 'inherited' by a kin of their late husbands. Many other women are required by custom to have unprotected sex with a so-called 'cleanser' who is said to 'rid' the widow of her late husband's spirit. The hapless woman risks contracting HIV/AIDS. No wonder in Kenya the incidence of HIV/AIDS is highest in certain regions. The man is a 'master' and the woman a 'chattel'.

In the Luo community, for instance, which is the second largest community amongst Kenya's 42 ethno-linguistic communities,—cultural factors have exacerbated HIV/AIDS prevalence. "Wife inheritance has increased HIV/AIDS prevalence and mortality-related cases... (the community) treat sex as a sacred act and is used as a tool to fulfil almost all cultural practices... Women are still treated as second rate to men. Thus their fate lies solely in the hands of men. ... Decisions are made for them. Thus during inheritance, the widow's estate management is executed by the clan." (Atinga Kwame JM; International Conference on AIDS; 15th: 2004: Bangkok, Thailand.)

In Somalia, which has suffered more than 20 years of conflict and anarchy, widows face more serious problems of survival. Large numbers of men have been killed during the war which continues to this day. The widows themselves were raped and tortured, and left with no way of taking care of themselves and their children. They also faced the ravages of HIV/AIDS.

In Afghanistan, thousands of women have been displaced owing to the continuing conflict there and in areas adjoining the borders with Pakistan. A UN report cited the dilemma of a widow who told IRIN (Integrated Regional Information Networks): "I am an educated woman, capable of earning for myself. But it would be considered immoral for me to live independently. Women live either with their parents or their husbands," said Uzma Farooq Khan, 25, a teacher from Mingora who later moved to Peshawar. "This makes it hard for widows to find a safe place to live while most are also illiterate and have no means of earning an income."

Khan is one of as many as two million war widows—well above 20 per cent of the female population—about whom there was hardly any real information, especially with regard to their "conditions in which they and their children are forced to live", according to UNIFEM. They have to struggle not only for their survival but also for their identity.

Typically, a widow's family is also more likely to go hungry and suffer extended illnesses. Assets such as land are more likely to be lost, and children are less likely to go to school. The loss of village men and extended family members aggravates a widow's situation and destroys her social safety net. Besides, she suffers from ill-health and malnutrition.

In Ghana's Ashanti and in other ethnic groups, widows are expected to undergo rituals like being secluded in the dark during the period of mourning, bathing in cold water, and abstaining from eating certain foods. They are harassed by their husbands' relatives who often disinherit them and their children. There are laws but many widows are unable to seek legal recourse because of various restrictions. In one reported case, the in-laws murdered a widow after she complained to a human rights lawyer that her brother-in-law had sold all of her husband's land, upon which she depended for food.

A report on gender issues in Ghana prepared for the Institute of Development Studies, at the University of Sussex, in Brighton, UK (cited by Immigration and Refugee Board of Canada) reveals: "Widows are often expected under customary law to undergo lengthy periods of mourning (of up to one year) whereas widowers generally only observe mourning for a few days. There may be restrictions on their movements, the imposition of food taboos and subjection to various forms of humiliation and abuse. Whilst these practices are traditionally considered as a form of rehabilitation, some of the practices involved are cruel, degrading and traumatic for the victims and amount to a denial of their rights" (UNECA, 1984: 7). They may also prevent women from engaging in normal economic activities, causing them considerable hardship. Bortei-Dorku (1990) reports that (as of 1990) the Law Reform Commission was considering legislation to abolish or restrict widowhood rites.

Older women members of extended families or communities have been known to be savagely brutalised and murdered, often on the basis of accusations of witchcraft (Ampofo, 1993; Baden et al. Jan 1994).

According to a report published by Empowering Widows in Development (EWD) on the situation of widows in Ghana, "what determines the widow's future is how tradition is interpreted at the local level. The practices of communities which are mainly traditionalist and Muslim are the most severe on widows..."

Among the northern tribes, widows are required to stay indoors. They are stripped naked and are handed leaves to maintain their modesty. The hapless women must then sit on a reed mat for days together or even weeks. They are also expected to hold a *calabash* (symbol of a dead husband) every time they leave the hut.

Widows may not cook and must eat and drink only from a special bowl to avoid polluting others. The corpse of the man is put in another part of the hut and the widow can visit it only in the company of an older woman.

After the burial, and once the cause of death is established by a soothsayer, the widows are led out naked and made to drink a special brew. They have to wash themselves in a designated place, usually a little used area where rubbish is thrown. Then their heads are shaved. The funeral ceremonies can be carried out in three days, but can last several weeks, months or even years depending on the wealth relatives possess.

Some of the mourning rites may include "ritual cleansing" through sex with designated individuals. These could be the "first stranger met on the road", or brothers-in-law, or the family heir. These coercive acts and others such as scarification (scarring) with unclean instruments are life threatening as well as degrading.

Ghana is the only country in the world that has attempted to eliminate such humiliation through legislation. The 1989 amendment to the Penal Code criminalises any act compelling a widow to undergo customs or practices that are cruel, immoral, or grossly indecent.

Mental and Physical Violence

Yet, according to EWD's partner groups, no one has ever been arrested and brought to court under this law. The problem stems from the fact that an illiterate and isolated rural widow would be hardly able to use this law even if she knew about it. "Physical and mental violence, including sexual violence and rape, is a common accompaniment of widowhood. Sometimes, as part of the mourning rite or some of the ceremonies (for example, having to sit naked and being left alone and destitute), widows are frequently vulnerable to extreme sexual abuse...

"The mental anguish, caused by such physical abuse, the sudden destitution, homelessness, starvation and insults, lead a number of widows to suicide. No investigation has yet been carried out to determine the numbers. In any case, the suicide of a widow is usually made to look like an accident.

"After the funeral ceremony, the widow is expected to choose the man she would like to marry. In practice though she may have no real choice; if a man succeeds in sleeping with the widow he will tell a close relative and the man then takes the widow as his wife. Any children she bears subsequently will be deemed as children of the dead husband. This is what is called a "levirate" union.

"In the Bolga district of the Upper East Region of Ghana, widows of fertile age are forced to continue to produce children in the name of the dead husband for the 'levir' and then often find themselves abandoned once they have given birth. They are at the mercy of the levir's other wife or wives.

They might say, as they did to one informant, 'You have killed your husband. Now you wish to kill mine'."

The Widows' Ministry (MOW), a Christian welfare organisation in Bolga, reports that so many widows are left caring for children conceived in this manner that they are unable to care for them adequately or feed them at all. Many widows faced with this situation turn to begging or prostitution. Or they are forced to abandon their babies and children. The young widow stares at a bleak future.

In many societies, widows are accused of bringing bad luck. A woman surviving her husband is suspect, and to avoid such suspicion she must demonstrate her grief and penance by wearing special clothes, avoid people and all social occasions such as weddings and parties.

In many communities, relatives would cast aspersions on the woman's character, claiming that she was a prostitute, or wasn't the rightful wife. These are tactics to circumvent the moral responsibility of supporting her and the legal commitment of letting her inherit her husband's property. In Ghana and some other African countries, it is said that such a reaction is often the result of the widow's refusal to accept a levirate or remarriage with one of the husband's male relatives.

A Christian minister in Ghana quoted by the UNHCR says that one young widow, unable to bear the jibes and accusations, locked herself up in a room with her baby. When someone eventually forced open the door he found she had hanged herself. The baby was still alive and was trying to suck from the dead mother's breast—she had fallen off the hook from the rafter above. He said that other Christian widows who refuse to follow harmful and degrading mourning rites or take another man from among the male relatives are accused of being 'haughty'. Some are labelled as witches.

In many instances, prostitution is often the only means of survival, but these widows often die early from HIV/AIDS and other associated illnesses. TB is a big problem. Widows never have enough money to buy medicines or follow a healthy diet.

An interview of a widow conducted by the researcher of the Widows Research Report (2009) also found that in developing countries even securing a job did not necessarily make a widow happier—a fact corroborated by the testimony of a Bangladeshi garment worker who was widowed in 2008. Salma (name changed), a garment factory worker in Dhaka in her mid-20s, whose husband was killed in a factory fire, gave the following account during a campaign seeking to raise awareness about the exploitative conditions under which workers produced clothes for the OECD market.

"We work from 8 am to 10 pm with only a 15-minute break. Work pressure is high. There is no time to go to the toilets, which are very dirty and few in number. There is no safe water to drink, while some have caught typhoid from it. We are often not paid on time, and overtime pay is sometimes not paid at all even when it is due. I earn £25 a month, £40 if I am in luck through overtime.

"Workers do not get maternity leave. Factories sometimes have very bright lights or do not have enough light. It becomes extremely hot inside the factory, with hardly any windows, which in any case are very small. And again, there is nothing to drink. We do not have protective gear to handle chemicals. [Air-borne particulate matter from the cloth is also a significant respiratory hazard if not controlled.]

"The buyers require two things of factory owners for the workers: a canteen and a children's day-care facility. But in my factory, we are not allowed to use them. In fact, we are told that if someone does ask where the children are we are to say that we have no children and so we don't need the children's facility."

A trade unionist representing Salma said that the wages these widows earn cannot support a family. So they are forced to live in slums, which, in the case of Dhaka, are located far from the factories. When the factory workers, 85 per cent of whom are women, agitated, not for a living wage, but for at least equal pay with men, some local Mullahs (Islamic clerics) trashed the concept of pay parity, saying if granted, the women would apparently "burn in hell".

On top of this, buses are not affordable on a daily basis, so the women are forced to walk (a two-hour walk one way), which means that if they have a late evening at work they are exposed to the risk of sexual assaults on their way home. Owing to the working conditions, workers spend no more than six to ten years in the industry.

Salma was able, through the trade unions, which fought her case, to get compensation for the death of her husband. As she is widowed, and the factory does not allow the use of the childcare facility, Salma's son, her only child, lives with her parents in the countryside. Salma gets to see her son only twice a year, usually during Eid.

Without her husband, she is locked into a vicious poverty trap. She was not asked if she wanted to remarry, which, in any case, would have been difficult because she has a child. Without remarrying and with only one young child as a possible source of future support she already faces the risk of deeper deprivation and the possibility of destitution.

Even widows whose husbands have left them some money are not immune to problems they unwittingly end up facing. Kidan Felomon, an Eritrean widow, thought she might be one of the luckier ones until events proved otherwise. "I am a 47-year-old widow and I live in Asmara, the capital of Eritrea. I have nine children. The oldest is 20 and the youngest is seven. My husband died of AIDS in 1999. He was a well-to-do merchant who travelled between Eritrea and Ethiopia.

"He did not tell me that he was infected with AIDS. Three years before his death I asked the doctor who was looking after him to tell me the cause of his sickness and he told me that my husband was suffering from liver cancer. But later, one of the nurses told me that my husband was infected with the virus.

"When I found out that I was HIV-positive too, I felt like killing my children and myself. The illness of my husband had impoverished our family. I sold all our furniture and jewellery to support my family and pay for my husband's medical expenses. I had 70 to 80 grams of gold, which my husband had bought for me, but I had to sell that too.

"There were times when I could not give food to my children. Once, my children went without food for a whole day. In the evening I gave the last plate of pasta to my husband and did not know what to give to the children..."

In Cambodia, the report found that widows did not suffer from the levels of gender discrimination seen in sub-Saharan Africa, South Asia and the Middle East, thanks to the reciprocal nature of kinship practices between the respective families of husbands and wives. This means even married daughters are able to assist their widowed mothers on the mothers' agricultural holdings, an unlikely scenario, for instance, in northern India.

However, Cambodia still provides a prime example of large-scale deprivation among widows, a corollary of widespread poverty in the country induced by economic underdevelopment. During the Vietnam war, a significant portion of the country was carpet-bombed and its land sown with landmines. Vast swathes of land thus couldn't be used fruitfully for livelihood.

The report pointed out that Cambodia "is one of the 49 countries designated by the UN as 'least developed' (Least Developed Country—LDC)". Around 80 per cent of the population is rural and widows in rural areas are reported to be unable to support their children through agriculture, thus calling for a diversified livelihood strategy. However, unlike the situation in Afghanistan, widows have been able to move into jobs men have traditionally held following the post-conflict shortage of men.

In Nairobi, when Susan Wagitangu's parents died, her brothers inherited the family land. "My sister and I didn't inherit," says Wagitangu, a 53-year-old Kikuyu woman. "Traditionally, in my culture, once a woman gets married, she does not inherit from her father." The assumption is that once a woman is married off she will be given land where she gets married. This did not apply to Wagitangu. When her husband died, her brothers-in-law forced her off her homestead and took away her cattle.

Wagitangu now lives in a Nairobi slum. "Nairobi has advantages," she says. "If I don't have food, I can scavenge in the garbage dump." (Human Rights Watch interview with Kenyan widow Susan Wagitangu, Nairobi, Oct 29, 2002).

Indeed, obscurantist traditions, religious interdictions and out-dated social practices are graver problems. Many widows lead a life worse than that of a pariah on the street, with no home to call their own, no sustainable source of income, and more often than not, forced to suffer utter ignominy. A few stories are gathered here to illustrate the lives of shame and humiliation that widows are forced to endure.

According to the findings of the 2009 Report, "Ultimately, each of the consequences represents a deprivation that requires immediate action, because if left unaddressed, negative ethical and economic costs, both of which are interlinked, will be felt by societies around the world. As a result, there are implications for the world's ability to achieve the Millennium Development Goals (MDGs)."

The survey carried out by Risto F. Harma for the Report, which examined all the aspects of discrimination and denial of even basic human rights to widows, affirmed the consequences of widowhood illustrated by examples given here. Poverty, health risks, social marginalisation and deprivation become central to their story.

"The big-picture view of the prevalence and severity of loss of income for widows as a group, from premature male death, is provided by a rare multi-country poverty study by Narayan et al (200). This study on causes and processes of poverty asked individual men and women around the world about the causes or 'triggers' of ('downward mobility') into poverty. Data in the study were ordered by the broad geographic groupings of 'Africa, Asia, Eastern Europe and Central Asia, and Latin America and the Caribbean'."

On the causes for slipping into poverty, (all regions combined), 43 per cent of widows cited "illness, injury, or death" as the primary cause, as compared to only 23 per cent of men. For men and women together, overall, "illness, injury, or death" was the most common out of the 17 poverty triggers the study recorded.

Nearly 35 per cent of men and 20 per cent of women reported "loss of employment or fewer opportunities", including "a decline in temporary and seasonal wages" as the reason for their falling into poverty. "The impact of the loss of husband's income on his death is a straightforward issue. The income he once earned was no longer available for the surviving wife and any dependent children... The severity of the impact of this material change in circumstances depends on whether women can take up paid employment, and if so, whether they enjoy wage parity with men. In many countries, women, in particular widows, are either not permitted to take up paid employment, or find it difficult to obtain it. Even where they do, they are paid less than men, sometimes significantly so" (Widows Research Report, 2009).

A new dimension has been added to the tragedy of widowhood following an alarming rise in their numbers in the wake of wars, ethnic cleansing and genocide, HIV/AIDS, terrorism and other conflicts.

A report for Rwanda found that "a minimum of 13 per cent of women and girls are widows (Rwanda Census 2002), with half of all married men slaughtered during the genocide". Risto also found that in the Democratic Republic of Congo, "sustained conventional and ongoing war has left some localities with a 40 per cent widowhood rate".

In Rwanda, it is also alleged that widows, who had suffered terribly during the genocide of 1994, were raped as part of state policy to spread the AIDS virus. It was part of the wider genocide plan. Chased, beaten, brutalised, raped, slaughtered or left as widows after the madness of the 100 days, these women have been struggling to rebuild their shattered lives. Fortuitously for them the Survivors Fund (SURF) volunteered to help by offering various services to widows, especially in dealing with HIV/AIDS.

However, the problem was compounded by sheer numbers. This is evident from the fact that SURF, which has been helping widows in rural areas, was forced to open two main centres to support well over 7,000 widows.

In 1998, a landmark decision by the International Criminal Tribunal for Rwanda (ICTR) declared rape as an act of genocide when it is committed with the intention of destroying a particular group. However, reports of conflicts between tribes in remote areas continue to come. Ethnic conflicts wreak havoc on women. Men are killed and widows raped and left to suffer.

In Kosovo, a small settlement called Meja is known as a village of widows. An extract from a diary maintained by Sherman Carroll, Director of Public Affairs, Medical Foundation, who took up a project for providing training in trauma counselling to post-graduate students of psychology at Prishtina University in Kosovo, is a telling narration of the misery widowed women endured there. (The project aimed to bolster mental health services for torture and war survivors in the UN protectorate.)

Stressing that the need for mental health services was crucial, Sherman wrote: "In a large field beside the road is a collection of graves. During the war, the villagers separated men from women. The women were taken away. Some 500 men and boys were shot here or nearby and their bodies buried. This is Kosovo's Srebrenica. When NATO bombed the Yugoslav army and its Serb militia back to Serbia, the crime scene was ethnically cleansed of its Kosovan dead. Now, some of the bodies have been returned from secret dumping grounds in Serbia. The graves are neatly arranged and tended, some one hundred of them. The field is marked out to receive the 400 bodies of the 'disappeared', who have not yet been returned to this scene of continuing crime."

Human Rights Watch and other organisations, such as the BBC, have reported on what has been called slaughter at Meja. The United Nations said there was little doubt that a mass killing took place in the village of Meja in the south-west of Kosovo. Possibly, Serb military forces shot 200 or more people. Lyndall Sachs of the United Nations refugee agency (UNHCR) says: "We have had successive waves of refugees who have passed through that area (Meja) and they have all spoken of bodies lying in ditches and in fields."

BBC reporters in northern Albania were also told by one group of refugees that Serb forces once stopped their convoy in Meja and forced up to 300 men to get out and stand in a small field. A second group of refugees who passed through the village later that day reported seeing a pile of bodies and 1,000 other Kosovan men sitting in rows under armed guard.

After 19 separate interviews with eyewitnesses who had passed through Meja, Human Rights Watch concluded that at least 100 men, and perhaps many more, between the ages of 16 and 60 were taken out of a convoy of refugees by Serbian forces and systematically executed in Meja on that day. The refugees who were interviewed had been systematically "cleansed" from neighbouring villages by Serbian special police, paramilitary units, and soldiers of the Yugoslav Army. The refugees were then forced to follow the road to Meja, which many of them passed through around midday. They reported seeing security forces holding "hundreds" of men at gunpoint. Those who passed through Meja later in the afternoon reported having seen a "large pile of bodies". All the area's men slaughtered, it was their widows who were the only survivors.

A key problem in research about widows is the unavailability of reliable statistics. In countries where wars have lasted for decades, such as Iraq, Iran, Cambodia or Vietnam, statistics about them are often inaccurate. However, a study by Susan H. Lee, called "The Long-Term Effects of War on Rural Cambodian Widows", reflects perceptively on their plight.

The tragic consequences of wars on women was portrayed by Barbara Sonneborn, who herself lost her husband in the Vietnam War. Sonneborn, years later, mustered courage to do something in memory of her husband. A photographer, she went on a "pilgrimage" to the country to make a documentary portraying the tragedy of women, both American and Vietnamese, who became widows. The documentary *Regret to Inform* won instant acclaim and was nominated for an Oscar.

The documentary recorded poignantly the stories of a dozen war widows, American and Vietnamese. A Vietnamese-American, Xuan Ngoc Nguyen, widowed in the fighting became a prostitute and said she used to have six American 'clients' a night. Nguyen also served as a translator for the documentary. Sonneborn is quoted by Peter M. Nichols in *Home Video: War Widows Relive Vietnam* as saying, "The common enemy was war."

State of Widows in Developed Countries

Even in the most developed and liberal Western societies widows complain of being ignored by friends who used to once welcome them when their husbands were alive. One of them said: "With couples around I feel unwanted."

Remarriage is, of course, permitted, as is cohabitation without marriage, but many widowed women, especially among the middle-class, report problems with married friends. One American widow—there are three widows to every widower aged 65—lamented that the trauma of loneliness, "of sleeping night after night alone in the bedroom" affected her mental and physical well-being.

"Social events, whether at homes or in public places, tend to be built around friendships with couples. Respondents complained that they heard about dinner parties to which they were not invited. Some widows explained it in terms of jealousy of married friends who did not want an extra woman around their husbands, or have a 'fifth wheel' around (Helena Znaniecki Lopata, *Widowhood in an American City*, 1973, page 151). She further pointed out that a "woman who has been established in a set of social roles usually experiences a disorganisation of this pattern (when husband was alive) immediately after her husband's death".

An in-depth study of widows in the West indeed shows that although they do not suffer from discrimination or cruel practices, they often do have a traumatic life, with little income or status. They too need attention from international forums and communities.

Such a scenario is brilliantly evoked in a book written by Alissa Toress, who was eight months pregnant when she lost her husband in the 9/11 atrocity. The outpouring of her grief in *American Widow* (Villard), a memoir about her first year as widow and single mother, is not only painful to read, but also brings to the fore the fact that the right to re-marry or gain financial security in the West does not necessarily heal the loss of a husband.

Widowhood is agonisingly painful. It needs to be treated as much as a social issue as an economic or human problem. Looking back at that first year after September 11, 2001, Torres writes, "We were constantly bombarded by the same images over and over: the burning towers. And I was bombarding myself with images of my husband. That's all I had. 9/11 was such a graphic event. Just writing about it wasn't enough. I needed to take control of the images."

From love between two young people, Toress takes us through her shock, pain, childbirth and the struggle to endure a great public tragedy and rebuild her life with her infant son.

Appalling Apathy

Such traumatic instances of widowhood notwithstanding, there is often complete apathy to their plight. Her husband dead, through no fault of her own, a woman can often undergo what is tantamount to inhuman treatment.

International bodies, NGOs, Governments and organisations like the Loomba Foundation have established that most of the 245 million widows worldwide live in misery and poverty and are open to exploitation.

The findings also reveal that the capacity of widows to cope with the impact of the death of their husbands depends largely on the social situation in which they live. Social conditions, especially in the developing countries, are not conducive to their welfare.

A report in 2008 by the International Women's Rights Action Watch notes: "The acceptance of, and sympathy for, widowers, but not for widows, is a situation that leads to the rejection of these women. Sometimes this rejection is mitigated by the extraordinary circumstances of widowhood, for example, war widows, but it is never excused. The hardship they face may be different but it still exists. If divorce is looked upon as the betrayal of one's promises, then widows, it must be assumed, have done no wrong. They have remained in the marriage till the death of their spouse."

The report touches on the fact that once they become vulnerable as single woman, widows are deprived of a life of dignity. "Very few find the support of the community or family." A widow laments: "How long would we have to live like worms of the earth?"

Some would gloss over this as perhaps the traditional lament of a grieving widow. Yet there are other instances which show how little is understood about a widow's psyche. In Nepal, for instance, when the government announced grants of 50,000 Nepali rupees (around £ 400) to single men who would marry widows and thereby help re-integrate them in the society, women from across the country marched to the capital Kathmandu to protest the 'humiliating' scheme.

The government justified it by saying that the scheme was necessary, in part, because of the 10-year-long civil war that claimed up to 13,000 lives and widowed many women. Such women are widely ostracised and discriminated against in the country.

Campaigners said the scheme would not only turn women into 'cash cows', but would also be open to abuse by people traffickers. They warned that in Nepal women were being traded for as little as Rs. 5,000. Lily Thapa, founder of the group Women for Human Rights (WHR) and one of the organisers of the rally, said: "It's totally humiliating for the women. We do not want this. It's against our human rights." Thapa also pointed out that widows in Nepal were routinely discriminated against, particularly in rural areas, and were prevented from wearing colourful clothes or attending important events as they were regarded as bearers of bad luck. "In the West you have no idea of the cultural code that exists here. If women want to wear colourful clothes it is their right."

The agitation continued for some time, with women marching through Kathmandu with banners declaring, "We don't want government dowries" and "Don't put a price on your mother". Ultimately, Nepal's Supreme Court blocked the scheme. A spokesman said, "The plan will promote greediness to marry widows and does not support or promote a healthy marriage system."

What Governments have mostly failed to accept is that legislations outlawing discrimination is over-ridden by religious laws, customs, and traditions at the local levels. In any case, widows, especially the millions of them in rural areas, are mostly ignorant of the legal rights they are entitled to.

The instances of war widows in developing countries who continue to suffer despite being given special allowances help illustrate this point, showing how such allowances are exploited. One survey found that generally a war widow who is given a pension and other assistance by the state is often forced to marry within her dead husband's family. The relative could already be married, but that is hardly any impediment. Once married, the widow is often neglected, while the original wife, the 'husband' and their children enjoy the financial aid that was supposed to support the widow.

Such instances were recorded in a report in November 2006

by the National Alliance of Women. "The monetary compensation given to war widows only worsened their situation as they were forced to remarry into the family of the dead husband for the sake of the money and then abandoned. The number of young widows is increasing as the HIV epidemic spreads."

The reality is that widows need different types of help depending on their social, cultural and economic situation. In the West measures have been initiated to 'rescue' them from a life of desolation, solitude and the trauma of losing a loved one. Various war widows' associations formed by women, most of them widows' themselves, have been doing commendable work in helping war widows. Governments too have several schemes for the welfare of war widows.

In the developing countries, too, there have been sincere and commendable endeavours to put an end to the social, physical and psychological torture widows undergo on account of barbaric customs and traditions. But these have not been enough. Referring to Kenya, the International Rehabilitation Council for Torture Victims (IRCT) says: "Violence against women, including rape and domestic violence, remains a serious concern. The work of human rights defenders is obstructed. Impunity is a problem although, legally, torture is prohibited under the Kenyan Constitution and the enactment of the Criminal Law Amendment Act in July 2003." The torture of widows is mostly under the guise of customary laws. And Kenya is not the only country to face such a problem.

An essay by Vanessa von Struensee (2005) "Widows, Child Marriage and AIDS" points out: "African widows still have a long way to go in the realisation of their rights. With increasing changes in the continent, a reformulation of existing rules and customary practices is inevitable. Economically, whole societies suffer as a result of continuing discrimination against widows. Furthermore, with the current source of HIV/AIDS in sub-Saharan Africa, debates about the rights and entitlements of widows take on new meaning." It further says that the problem of widows in Africa "cannot be divorced from the larger problems facing many Third World nations and, particularly, the problems of women, children, and other marginalised groups within these nations".

Who are Responsible for Widows' Miseries?

The plight of widows in developing countries and conflict-ridden countries clearly implicates institutional, public and private actors in the international context. Widows, as an exclusive category for attention, are "invisible to international bodies and even national Governments. They are bracketed with people who are poverty-stricken in the international economic system. They hardly matter in the secondary position allotted to economic and social rights in the human rights regime." Furthermore, legal and political apathy towards widows raises the issues of rural underdevelopment and the feminisation of rural poverty in the Third World.

The customs and rites relating to widowhood, as we have seen in the instances in the preceding pages, have imposed unspeakable hardships on widows. Women, in general, as it is, are vulnerable to traditional practices like female genital mutilation and ritual cleansing, especially in Africa.

Ritual cleansing has been studied at length in the research report. It is meant to "cleanse a widow for purposes of effective separation from her dead husband's spirit and re-admission into his family and consists of practices that risk HIV / AIDS infection. Cleansing takes all forms, including the widow's bathing or sleeping with the husband's body and the widow's having sexual intercourse with her brothers-in-law. It is worth noting that corollary cleansing of widowers does not go to similar extents."

In Ghana, the survey found some men actually "watch out" for widows trying to claim their inheritance and pretend to "marry" them. Having obtained their money they desert them. Under customary law, in Ghana as in Tanzania, widows have no rights to inheritance. In the patrilineal North, under customary law, the brothers of the dead man divide the estate among themselves. In the matrilineal South, inheritance goes through the mother's male siblings and sons.

It is apparent that notwithstanding the laws that seek to protect widows from barbaric rituals and social taboos, most of these women continue to suffer deprivation, disgrace and humiliation. Their case cannot be any more overstated, for along with their dependants, widows of the world account for a sixth of the world's population.

2

WILL THE WORLD EVER WIPE THE TEARS OF ITS WIDOWS?

You can tell the condition of a nation, by looking at the status of women

— JAWAHARLAL NEHRU

Widows are also 'women'. But they are seldom treated thus. The moment their husbands die, widows lose their protector, their status and are discriminated against and deprived of all that they were entitled to as a woman. This is the worst possible crisis of their lives. Worse, this is not something exclusive to any one culture, society or region but is spread across most parts of the world.

The deprivation, amounting to serious human rights violations, and characterised as "harmful traditional practices" by the United Nations, affects not only widows, but also have cascadent effects upon their dependants. All together, they account for nearly a billion people, or a sixth of the world's population. By the Nehru yardstick, the state of the world is clearly alarming and distressful.

One of the main reasons why widows continue to be subjected to gross human rights violations is that although they number 245 million, there has been no comprehensive research or attempt to gather information on a global scale about their existence. This is possibly because once a widow, she literally *ceases* to be a woman and is in fact treated like an outcast in most developing countries.

The United Nations report "Women 2000", put together following the Beijing Declaration, acknowledged that widows were actually absent from the statistics of many developing countries and were rarely mentioned in the multitude of reports on poverty, development, health or human rights published in the last 25 years. "The growing evidence of their vulnerability, both socio-economic and psychological, now challenges many conventional views and assumptions about this 'invisible' group of women." It is in these countries, neglected in surveys, that widows have suffered the worst inhuman outrages.

The absence of wide-ranging, in-depth inquiries about the tormented lives of this 'invisible' group of women, has also been largely to blame for the failure of international organisations to classify them as a separate category, in need of special focus and efforts.

The 'invisibility' of widows is instructive. In most societies in developing countries, women die a social death with the demise of their husbands.

"The less you find, the more telling it becomes about a much undervalued population," says Eileen Stillwaggon, reacting to the absence of research into the plight of widows.

Little information, in English, the language of most international organisations, has been available, for instance, on widows in East Asia or the Middle East or for that matter in OECD (Organisation for Economic Cooperation and

Development) countries. The majority of references found were about widows in sub-Saharan Africa or South Asia. Those too were limited to areas where researchers or NGOs were focused on.

Searches on the Internet for an association or charity working for widows, in, say, Rwanda, Kenya or Uganda threw up little information. In fact, no information, backed with data, about widows in Africa can be found in any one place.

It is safe to assume that if international bodies had carried out a proper census, gathering detailed information about the state of the widows and their children in developing countries, the measures taken by them for gender equality and eradication of poverty and discrimination could have been far more effective and inclusive. They would have realised that widows and their children needed special attention.

"The woefully inadequate information on a global scale about the social and economic sanctions and barbaric rituals widows are subjected to has hampered several agencies of the United Nations that have been focused on many humanitarian causes—poverty, health, deprivation, literacy and discrimination—to help them." (Widows Research Report, 2009)

The forty-sixth session of the Commission on the Status of Women, held in March 2002 at the UN Headquarters in New York, considered the following two thematic issues:

- Eradicating poverty including through the empowerment of women throughout their life cycle in a globalising world
- Environmental management and mitigation of natural disasters: A gender perspective

In theory, though widows would be covered by the clause "eradicating poverty including through the empowerment of women..." the reality on the ground has been that widows, after having been abandoned by their families and communities, are seldom able to benefit from any such schemes. Treated as pariahs, they suffer from the 'sins of omission' as the UN has itself conceded. In addition, the mindset of people and societies is also such that widows are hardly *allowed* to exert their rights. The resultant predicament of widows does not weigh on the conscience of society.

Even world organisations like Empowerment and Development of Women (EDW) have so far sought to help widows only in a few select regions. Again, credit must go to NGOs and women's associations who have been working for and helping widows in these regions. It is these organisations that have brought to light the plight of widows.

Some of these NGOs have done commendable work in helping widows and their children on the ground. However, such work is obviously limited in the scale of its impact for want of resources. These NGOs also often find themselves isolated politically by vested interests. Often they do not have the wherewithal to tackle the customs and traditions that have shackled the destinies of the widows.

Although war widows have been given support by governments there has been no survey to assess how much they have in reality benefited from schemes meant to rehabilitate them after the loss of their husbands. Often the women have been deprived of the welfare schemes meant for them. In fact, though army establishments in many countries have special departments looking after grants for war widows, it is impossible for them to monitor how much of the assistance given has actually reached or helped them.

The woeful lack of data on widows across the world has had other consequences too. For instance, there has been no survey on how much the legal and welfare measures taken by several individual governments—such as those of India, Ghana or Uganda—have helped in rescuing widows from their humiliating existence. A few NGOs and academics have, in their regions, studied the impact of the measures carried out by governments. Their studies have shown that legislation has largely failed to help the illiterate, impoverished widows or even the better-off widows in communities and societies which have fostered oppressive and obscurantist traditions. "The appalling treatment just entrenches the cycle of poverty and deprivation," said Cherie Blair, "because if the mother has no money, the children are pulled out of school. With no education, they are doomed to spend their lives in the most menial jobs if they get work at all."

In many tribal societies, widows must marry a kin of their deceased husbands. Such practices violate the human rights of widows but most governments hesitate to come down heavily on such 'traditions' and 'customs'. Understandably, governments have found it complicated and difficult to carry out systemic social reform. Indeed, it may not be possible for governments alone to legislate social reform for many officials in governments have been reared in societies or communities that have fostered such regressive practices.

These historical wrongs perpetrated on widows have never been computed on a global scale, with little world attention, therefore, being drawn to the inhuman existence of these nearly one billion 'humans'. The Loomba Foundation, which has been working for widows and their children in many developing countries, realised that unless worldwide data was available it would never be possible to help widows realistically and systematically. It took up the rather formidable task of inquiring into the state of widows in developing countries and also sought to study the needs of the widows in the West.

The survey and groundwork in collecting data and information for the report, *Widows Research Report* (2009), needed perseverance and patience because gathering details from across the world, especially from closed tribal and tradition-bound societies and communities reluctant to talk about the state of widows, was difficult and complex. Notwithstanding the hurdles, the report—the first ever to provide systematic information about widows globally—prepared painstakingly by the researcher Risto F. Harma, has been a ground-breaking one.

The survey, instigated by the Loomba Foundation, was carried out by World Public Opinion and facilitated by the Royal Institute for International Affairs (Chatham House). It was released in June 2008 and incorporated into the Widows Research Report, which was completed in September 2009. The Report covers 10 thematic areas and 45 topics, which need to be enquired into seriously.

The Report found that widows worldwide numbered 245 million, and not 100 million as estimated before this report. The enormous difference between the earlier presumption and the findings of the 2009 report is ample evidence of the extent of neglect of the lives of widows and their problems. The World Public Opinion survey covered developed and developing countries, and established that discrimination against widows is widespread, and therefore a global problem.

More importantly, the survey collected data on perceptions about how societies treated widows across a sample of 17 developed and developing countries. Nearly 63 per cent of the respondents reported that widows were given a far worse treatment than the general female population.

Widows Research Report also focuses on how illiteracy and poverty are the other factors that keep widows from seeking judicial help even when there are laws for protecting their rights. Seodhi's fate in Malawi is an apt example of the helplessness of widows. She said: "My children and I were kicked out of our home and beaten up by my brothers-in-law" (UN 2001:1).

Many such instances abound where these women continue to endure extraordinary harassment despite laws and state support. It reinforces the argument that the deprivations and distress widows face across the world need to be categorised as an international issue. The report presents national, regional and global statistics. The findings also starkly expose the social stigma attached to widows and people's attitude towards widowhood.

It also categorises widows according to the circumstances under which they lost their husbands. The categories include genocide, wars and regional conflicts, landmine explosions, farming, mining and industrial accidents, and epidemics like HIV / AIDS.

Widows Research Report tabulates the economic condition of these women who were widowed on account of each of the above-mentioned causes. It also studies abuse of child widows, child abuse, link to diseases and regional differences in their treatment.

The World Health Organisation, the World Bank and such world organisations reportedly do not have adequate information about widows in developing countries. The 2009 Report fills that information gap. It also documents the problems widows in affluent societies in developed countries face. The Report—detailed study of hitherto overlooked social issues with far-reaching negative impacts resulting from widows' and their children's deprivation—can help governments and international organisations to apply appropriate human rights conventions and laws and also target social and economic structures that have helped exploit and oppress widows.

More crucially, the Report has succeeded in separating widows and their dependants from the category of women and the poor in general by collating, for the first time, on a global scale, the circumstances widows find themselves in following the demise of their husbands. It thus provides information and data international agencies and people require to fully comprehend the plight of widows.

It also presents pointers to the future: That problems are multiplying and that their solutions are getting more complex with widows growing in number in the wake of wars and conflicts across the world and increasing incidence of HIV / AIDS in Africa.

By also enumerating the exploitation and sexual abuse of young widows, the 2009 Report brings to the fore the fact that it is a human rights issue, which is a self-declared priority area for the United Nations.

Following the comprehensive Loomba Foundation report, governments and international bodies cannot continue to gloss over the problems faced by the world's widows. The 2009 Report is the first definitive guide to the problems faced by impoverished widows and their children. But a solitary initiative by one Foundation, however meticulous, laudable and credible, may not necessarily help in convincing governments to come together and help the cause of the world's widows. The UN and its agencies must show resolve and take the lead.

The Loomba Foundation has been trying to convince the UN to take up the cause of widows and their problems as a fundamental human rights issue. The UN could help Trusts and NGOs registered with it to campaign for building public awareness, while helping to empower widows in their respective regions.

With a membership of 192 countries, the UN is the only body that can encourage and motivate governments, charities and foundations, or even multinationals, to take up the cause of widows and their dependants. The necessity to categorise them exclusively has been made possible by both this book and the Report commissioned by the Loomba Foundation.

The Loomba Foundation rightly chose to focus on the UN to impress upon it that its attention was needed for the resolution of the travails widows and their dependants have to endure. In other words, the problems widows face are universal. The differences lie only in degrees.

So far, despite their best efforts and intentions, Trusts and NGOs have, understandably, been unable to help resolve these problems. There are thousands of Seodhis in the developing world. The Widows Research Report showed that most governments either chose to ignore their grievances for fear of alienating large segments of people who cling to old beliefs and taboos, or then took half-hearted measures. In effect, this lackadaisical attitude has helped perpetuate the abuse of widows.

"Only the likes of the UN, and its agencies and the European Union, who have been focusing on development in the Third World, can really help by persuading their member-states to bring into focus jointly the inhuman treatment of widows," said Raj Loomba, Founder, Loomba Foundation. "They alone can motivate and to some extent convince governments to take up the cause of widows and come down heavily if under the sheen of culture, custom or faith they are deprived of their status and rights. A joint, universal campaign is required."

Many governments have, in fact, tried but failed to change social and tribal laws. More crucially, they have been unable to exert any influence on people's mindsets in their respective countries.

In the West, the problem is not as appalling, for it is largely a psychological one, resulting out of loneliness and emotional trauma. Widows in the developed world do not suffer from the weight of age-old customs or beliefs. In fact, they have the option of remarrying and are often also supported by social welfare schemes. Moreover, statistics about them are available in the respective countries.

However, an Australian study, cited in the Widows Research Report, noted that in most research in the country, "little emphasis has been given to the broader needs of these women..." beyond the personal meaning and psychological effects of losing a husband (Feldman 2002: 135). But with the growing number of old widows, the problem in these countries is also becoming complex.

The UN and its agencies, even governments, have the example of the Foundation's campaign to create global awareness about the neglect of widows. The Foundation has launched an international advocacy campaign to enlist the support of internationally known personalities and a few governments, especially in African countries.

The Foundation gave a further boost to the understanding of the problem by launching International Widows Day on June 23 in 2005. Besides Yoko Ono and other prominent speakers, organisations working for the welfare of widows in 10 different countries, including Pakistan, Nigeria, Rwanda and Bangladesh, also attended the first conference in London.

The curse of widowhood was highlighted for the first time. The response was so encouraging that since then June 23 has been observed as International Widows Day in several countries. Many individuals and corporations were acquainted of the need to rescue widows and their dependants from the hell they have been living in. A number of them have volunteered to assist in the Foundation's campaigns. In fact, the Foundation also took upon itself the responsibility of training widows in different vocations. It has provided funds to a number of widows in India and Africa to help them start their own businesses. In Delhi, several widows were skill-trained. One was helped to set up a boutique in her own in-laws' house. She is happy to be independent and a contributor to the family's budget.

The Loomba Foundation, in collaboration with the Commonwealth Games Organising Committee and the Heart Foundation, also hosted a health check-up camp for 100 widows and their children on World Health Day on April 7, 2010.

The Foundation collaborated with Oxfam and the Prince's Trust too to reach remote areas in Rwanda. Individual enterprises like the ones undertaken by the Foundation have done tremendous work. A farming co-op of AIDS-affected widows and orphans in rural Rwanda is working towards rehabilitating 100 families headed by women or children. Besides, the Foundation is also assisting over 1,600 local orphans and disabled people.

Another organisation, Bringing Hope to the Family (BHF), has been operating in the district of Kyenjojo and other nearby districts in western Uganda. The project has been working with nearly 100 children and 27 widows. It is noteworthy that they started out without any capital and operated on faith donations. Seeing the good work being carried out by BHF, authorities and charity organisations helped them build 10 homes for orphans and widows. If the UN commits itself to rescuing widows then more such commitments can come from multinationals, major corporations and charities.

In Tanzania, the Tanzania Widow Women Association (TAWIWO) run by two widows has been working to promote social and economic well-being of widows in the country. It also provides technical and financial assistance and advice to the women.

It was against all odds that the two widows ventured to help other widows who were too poor or handicapped to fight the circumstances brought about by their bereavement. Evelimy Ngokho, a former accountant of the National Bank of Commerce, founded TAWIWO, while Ruth B. Magesse, a mother of three and a professional accountant who worked with CRDB Bank, joined forces to fight for the rights of women. Funds poured in once the sincerity of their purpose, and scale of the problem were understood.

The positive outcome of such enterprises shows how quickly widows could be empowered to sustain themselves and command respect, albeit grudgingly, in their community. Although such endeavours by individual organisations are praiseworthy, it has to be pointed out again that until international bodies, which have reach and resources, and influence over governments and financial institutions, take up the issue of widows, it is impossible to truly tackle a global issue.

The UN has recognised that "it can be said there is no group more affected by the sins of omission than widows..." (UN 2001: 2). However, such a candid admission has so far only led to partial and porous help through its agencies in select regions. For instance, the Empowerment of Widows in Development (EWD), founded by Margaret Owen and set up to lobby the cause of widows in developing countries at the local, national and international levels, has been able to monitor the state of widows in just 10 countries—Nigeria, Zambia, Mozambique, Zimbabwe, Ghana, Malawi, Bangladesh, Tanzania, India and Uganda. However, EWD has been doing its best.

According to the revised estimates of the now famous "one-dollar-a-day" measure of extreme poverty by the World Bank (now using $1.25 a day), in 2005, 1.4 billion people around the world live in extreme poverty—where basic needs are not met (World Bank 2008b). Another 2.6 billion live in moderate poverty on two-dollars-a-day. Loomba Foundation's report shows that in 2010, there will be almost 60 million widows around the world living in extreme poverty. Another 57.4 million widows live in moderate poverty of two-dollars-a-day, where some basic needs are met, but they are still at risk of falling into extreme poverty. In total, there are 116.7 million widows across the globe who live in poverty due to various causes—which means 47 per cent of all widows.

Even in the West, widows with low educational qualifications live lives of extreme insecurity for they can neither access affordable healthcare nor secure reasonably well-paid jobs. As President Barack Obama said that many Americans were, "one medical emergency away from bankruptcy". Something that is true of most developing countries as well.

Owen (2002) while observing that "Widowhood has a severe impact on its victims," also agreed that "few of the international agencies working in development and poverty reduction are directly concerned with helping widows".

In her *Widows for Peace and Democracy*, Owen pointed out that it was "essential that governments and UN entities specifically focus on the particular situation of widows if the MDGs (Millennium Development Goals) have any realistic chance of being realised.

"The poverty and exclusion of widows recycles and expands the poverty trap to embrace all those dependent on them with irrevocable consequences for society as a whole.

Neglecting the impact of marginalised widowhood frustrates all of the eight goals of the MDGs and their targets.

"Children of widows are withdrawn from school, widow poverty, through lack of legal rights to inheritance, land and property, forces widows and their daughters into economic exploitation including child labour, prostitution and trafficking. Inhuman and degrading burial and mourning rites help to spread AIDS."

She further said: "Never before has the female population in many developing countries known so many widows. In the aftermath of conflict, in the context of AIDS, estimates for some countries suggest that over 60 per cent of all women are widows or wives of the missing and 70 per cent of children dependent on destitute women without male breadwinners.

"Yet none of the major donors (EU, DFID, USAID) nor any of the UN agencies has supported initiatives to redress the poverty and human rights abuses suffered by this group of women. The exception is SIDA (Sweden)."

She is right. Widows have so far been bracketed with the poverty-stricken, but no succour is possible till traditional and social attitudes towards them change or they are viewed as a separate and distinct issue, rather than simply as 'women'. For reasons explained above, they seldom are beneficiaries of any relief. Their own families and communities are major obstacles. "Unaware of her rights and incapable of asserting herself, a woman has no recourse to judicial help," Owen added.

The problem is that international bodies have so far grouped them with women in general while computing poverty. Consequently, as observed earlier, the problems widows face simply do not figure on the agenda of most international forums.

Poverty as a human rights issue has received consistent attention. It is enshrined in the UN's International Covenant on Economic, Social and Cultural Rights. However, few have exclusively addressed its dire consequences on widows and their children. Naturally, there has been no exclusive provision for them.

Yet for the majority of widows globally, day-to-day poverty is the defining issue that makes all other outrages possible with such ease. Widowhood stigmatises their social position and institutionalises the indignities they face.

Human rights specialist Prof. Joshua Castellino argued that the 1979 UN Convention on the Elimination of All Forms of Discrimination Against Women (CEDAW) specified "the elimination of all forms of discrimination against women", which, therefore, covers widows. He went on to point out that law sets the standard and acts as "a statement of intent", to be followed by action on the ground to help change social attitudes. This is important if the attitude towards widowhood is to change. On the ground, however, little has changed except in limited areas where charities or NGOs have been campaigning for widows' rights and fighting against their oppression.

There have been thus far four UN World Women's Conferences—in Mexico in 1975, in Copenhagen in 1980, in Nairobi in 1985, and in Beijing in 1995. Were widows given any forum or attention? No. Even more telling is the fact that although CEDAW was ratified by many countries widows find mention only in the category of the aged.

It can be argued that under the 12 critical areas the 1995 Beijing Platform for Action resolved to address—among them being poverty, violence to women, the female children, health, education, employment, women and armed conflict, institutional mechanisms, and human rights—widows would invariably be covered. However, they hardly find any mention. Thus they can never be beneficiaries in most developing countries. Also, as repeatedly pointed out, between widows and all aid legitimately due to them stand their families and communities.

"When their husbands die, widows in developing countries rarely have the right to inherit property or have their rights enforced. They are frequently evicted from their property, their possessions taken from them, and often their children are also removed from their care and protection," says EWD on its website.

Owen, who also presented *A World of Widows* at the 1995 Beijing Fourth United Nations Conference on Women, identified the myth believed by many in the West that widows in developing countries were supported by their extended families and adult sons, as well as local customs. The testimony of the widows at the conference clearly revealed the brutal realities widows the world over live through, highlighting the failure of civil law, religion, and custom to protect women whose husbands have died.

The testimony of the widows at this meeting also revealed the tragic reality of their lives, highlighting the failure of civil law, religion, and custom to protect women whose husbands have died. The consensus at the meeting was that discrimination against widows was so severe that action must be taken to bring their situation to the attention of the world. Who can do that? Who else, but the United Nations.

Raj Loomba stressed, "The UN has to take up the cause of widows". It can find some of the truths about widows in developing countries that are listed at EWD's website (www.widowsrights.org/).

Three fundamental facts the website points out can be listed briefly:

- That, most widows live in severe poverty;
- Even where laws exist to protect women whose husbands have died, widows are generally not aware of their rights;
- Even when they are, the courts are often controlled by local customs that give all property to the women's in-laws, or their rights are lost in the confusion generated by the conflicting systems of family, local, religious and civil custom, all of which are patriarchal in conception and organisation.

This reinforces the need to consider and address their

conditions separately. Ways and means have to be devised to ensure that aid meant for the widows actually reaches them. The Loomba Foundation Report, in fact, lays out such a roadmap.

Even a cursory study of the Report would reveal to the UN that widows have continued to be poor and are also *kept* poor despite several schemes designed by its agencies to foster gender equality and bring succour to the poverty-stricken. The Report illustrates this by revealing that communities in South Asia continue to grab property that legitimately belongs to widows. This makes it evident that despite laws protecting their inheritance rights these hapless women are unable to benefit from them. Such denial of benefits to widows can be redressed only if they are categorised separately.

A World Health Organisation report of 2001 supported this argument: "Very few governments and NGOs view widows as a special category with individual problems and special status."

After the Report's findings, there cannot be any reason for the failure of the UN or any other international forum to understand that widowhood is as much a human problem as poverty in general, ethnic cleansing or HIV/AIDS. The Report and this book show clearly that widowhood is a challenging issue that has to be taken up on a priority basis. "There is no time to be lost," says Raj Loomba.

This book, based on the findings of the Report, has also analysed reasons for the absence of mainstream attention on the question of widows. As pointed out earlier, widows in developing countries are treated as outcasts and are at the mercy of their relatives. Some governments, including India, Ghana, Rwanda and Kenya, legislated schemes to help them. But these legislations have mostly failed to transform people's perspectives.

This is evident from some instances from Ghana and Uganda where strict laws against any form of discrimination have been in place for quite some time. "Customary laws and practices have continued to be in force largely due to the lack of political will to confront issues of inequality and discrimination in a holistic and comprehensive manner..." noted the *International Journal of Law, Policy and Family*, pointing out the failure of the Women's Rights to Equality and Non-Discrimination in Ugandan legislation in helping women.

Painting widows as witches is a rampant practice in many tradition-bound societies. According to a report by Help Age International in Tanzania, about 500 older women, mostly widowed because of AIDS related diseases or by the death of AIDS affected husbands, were stoned to death or deliberately killed in 2000.

There are deeply ingrained cultural, religious and financial factors that hamper enforcement of laws or affect the ability of widows to access the courts of law. Millions of women in tribal areas in Africa are unaware of their rights and the recourses available to them.

Luckily in recent years, in a few Indian villages or remote areas where NGOs have either been active or where women a little more literate, widows have gradually been able to assert their rights. In India, for example, the compulsory representation of women in panchayats (rural bodies that adjudicate on local issues) has helped significantly.

Why is there such callous disregard towards the problems that the widows of the world face? To reiterate, the primary cause for such an indifferent approach at all levels, but more significantly at international forums, is that women in most societies lose their identity as individuals once their husbands die.

"The casualness with which the problems of widows are treated is a callous violation of human rights. It might not be wrong to believe that people who could help are ignorant (or choose to be ignorant) about the pitiable state of widows," observed a 60-year-old widow living in a shelter. She did not wish to be identified.

A report by the UK Department for International

Development noted, "Significant attention has been paid to women's needs and rights in adulthood, particularly during their child-bearing years ... [but] more still needs to be done, however, to fully understand the challenges posed by abrupt changes in status brought about widowhood."

Children of widows can seldom afford to go to school and often suffer from ill-health and stunted growth owing to malnutrition. They are forced to beg or are exploited as child labour. Girls are generally pushed into under-age marriages, or are trafficked or sold, and sexually abused. Tragically, they often join the ranks of the HIV/AIDS infected.

However, there has been no detailed information, country- or region-wise about the economic status of widows and its effect on their children. Nothing was thus available about child abuse and exploitation either. This was remedied by the Widows Research Report, 2009.

This book also demonstrates, with examples, that widows continue to be 'non-existent' as far as rehabilitation or employment schemes are concerned.

The 'sins of omission' have also adversely affected young widows whose numbers have increased substantially. Wars, ethnic cleansing and conflicts in large parts of the world—Mozambique, Angola, Somalia, Cambodia, Vietnam, Uganda, Rwanda, Sierra Leone, Bosnia, Kosovo, Sri Lanka (until recently), East Timor, Guatemala and Afghanistan—have widowed the young and the old alike. Tales of rapes, homelessness and trauma abound—it is no longer a mere statistical issue.

The problem is that although young, widows in many societies are barred from remarrying. If they do, they are often forced into unions that generally lead them to a hellish existence. Yet no comprehensive information is available either of the total number or about the condition of women widowed in the wake of violent outbreaks world over. We do know that two million have been widowed in Afghanistan so far, and at least 740,000 in Iraq (reported in the *New York Times*,

February 22, 2009) and 96,000 in Palestine (Loomba Foundation Widows Research Report estimate for 2010); in both cases, the predominant category of widows affected are young women and girls. A 2008 survey of Iraqi women by Oxfam, called "In Her Own Words", captures the hardships faced by Iraqi widows. It found that 76 per cent of all widows were not receiving the government widows' pension they were due, but little is known about the number widowed in Iraq or Palestine.

The number of young widows has risen substantially on account of the scourge of HIV/AIDS, especially in sub-Saharan Africa. It is said that because of biological reasons, women are twice as likely to contract AIDS as compared to men. According to reports the rates of infection among young women between the ages of 10 and 24 are five times higher than for young men in certain regions of Africa.

The other custom of child marriage, still prevalent in some developing countries also increases the number of child and young widows. Destined to face exploitation, sexual abuse and even trafficking, their problems are even worse.

A comprehensive solution to the problems widows face is possible only if the UN takes the lead in persuading all countries, especially the developing ones, to formulate a common programme of action for widows. Recognising officially June 23 as International Widows Day, (for which the Loomba Foundation has been campaigning), will help focus the world's attention on the problems widows face, across the globe.

The present time is indeed opportune as in several countries widows' issues are being taken up by the Loomba Foundation, the Prince's Trust and several women's organisations. Along with them, the UN can take up the resolution of widows' problems and adopt it as one of its major targets.

Widows for Peace and Reconstruction was also set up in August 2001 to represent the special needs of war widows and to ensure that their voices are heard in post-conflict peace building. However, a few instances mentioned in the earlier chapter show that there is a desperate need to ensure that war widows, most of whom are young, are not coerced into unwilling marriages, with a new 'husband' and his family stealing pensions or salaries that is rightfully the widow's.

The observation made by Margaret Owen that, "... Governments and UN entities specifically focus on the particular situation of widows if the MDGs have any realistic chance of being realised", is significant.

Considering the extent of suffering of widows, of which reports from most developing countries have already been compiled by the Loomba Foundation for reference, the need is for support from the UN to reinforce the reach, influence and capacity of widows' groups, societies, governments, institutions like the judiciary, and social workers and lawyers to act against the atrocities heaped on widows. This will ensure that the rights of widows and their dependants are protected and nurtured.

The UN has to take the lead on a priority basis to bring relief to the humiliated one-sixth of the world's humanity.

3

THE ROOTS OF THE TRAGEDY

Macabre manifestations of widowhood

A widow does not remain a woman for most families, communities and societies in most countries. The Widows Research Report (2009) studied to what degree widowed women were treated worse than other women in various countries. A WorldPublicOpinion.org poll of 17 nations around the world also confirmed that there was a widespread perception that widows and divorced women were treated worse than other women. In only two countries did a majority say that there was no discrimination against widows.

In 12 of the 17 nations polled, about 4 in 10 perceived that there was some or a great deal of discrimination against widows. On an average, across all 17 nations, just 29 per cent said there was no discrimination against widows at all, while

20 per cent said there was a little, 27 per cent some, and 16 per cent a great deal.

Raj Loomba, chairman of the Loomba Foundation, commenting on the findings said that widows' deprivation was an issue not exclusive to any culture, society or region. "The widows are treated worse than other women because of various reasons but primarily because of customs and extreme poverty."

"The discrimination against widows and divorced women appears to be a phenomenon in many countries, not just some traditional cultures," said Steven Kull, director of WorldPublicOpinion.org. "People in most countries, including developed ones, recognise there is at least some discrimination."

Loomba made a significant point by highlighting the risk widows face because of poverty. "Out of 245 million widows, nearly over 100 million live in extreme poverty leading to malnutrition, diseases and abuse. They are under extreme risk of getting HIV/AIDS. We are trying to convince the United Nations that it must focus on the poverty and plight of widows exclusively. They have continued to be extremely poor despite various schemes of the UN agencies for eradicating poverty especially in women and the aged."

The UN has to look at this aspect urgently. At the regional level, HIV/AIDS is the fourth leading cause of death in low and middle-income countries while the disease is the leading cause of death for most in the 15-59 age group in sub-Saharan Africa, according to the Widows Research Report, which quoted Lopez et al (2006), pages 69 and 71.

Manifestations of Poverty

The UN Rights Watch 2009 said a direct correlation between women's status, violations of their human rights and HIV transmission has been established. Unfortunately, as the Loomba-sponsored Widows Research Report showed, the percentage of poor widows, illiterate, oppressed and in bondage of customs is very high in developing countries. They are subjected to customary laws, heavily weighted against them.

In June 2001, UNIFEM Executive Director Noeleen Heyzer observed: "The reason why AIDS has escalated into a pandemic is because inequality between women and men continues to be pervasive and persistent. It is time for the AIDS community to join hands with the international women's community to hold governments accountable."

Sub-Saharan Africa

*Since the early 1980s, over 20 million have died of AIDS, most of them rather young, being under age of 35. Three-quarters of the persons estimated to be living with the disease worldwide are in sub-Saharan Africa. More than half of the people living with HIV/AIDS are women and girls.

*Women widowed by AIDS suffer the injustice of both statutory and customary laws... (they) do not figure in AIDS programme priorities. HIV/AIDS will cause many millions of African women to be widowed, and widowed at a younger age than would have been the case in its absence.

*Human rights abuses against women (especially the widowed) and girls that fuel HIV/AIDS in Africa are: (1) abuses targeting girls; (2) risks facing women and girls in long-term unions; (3) the effects of susceptibility to HIV/AIDS in terms of discrimination in property and inheritance rights; (4) persistence of at times deadly traditional practices; (5) the ways of treating sex workers exacerbate the epidemic; (6) the failure to properly address wartime rape and related abuses; (7) the failure to provide timely assistance to rape victims; and, (8) discrimination in access to basic health information and services. These topics are addressed in turn in the sections below.

*By the year 2020, the number of deaths from AIDS in Africa will approximate the number of deaths, military and civilian combined, in both the World Wars of the 20th century. Then it should also be said that a pronounced majority of those deaths would be women and girls. The toll on women and girls is beyond human imagination. "...it presents Africa and the world with a practical and moral challenge which places gender at the centre of the human condition. The practice of ignoring a gender analysis has turned out to be lethal... For the African continent, it means economic and social survival. For the women and girls of Africa, it's a matter of life or death." (Stephen Lewis, UN Secretary-General's Special Envoy on HIV/AIDS in Africa, July 2002)

*Women widowed by AIDS suffer the injustice of both statutory and customary law that militates against their ability to retain marital property. The stigma of AIDS often leads to their being abandoned or abused. The millions of children orphaned by AIDS face a stunning array of human rights abuses, many of them more frequent and deadly among girls than boys. (Human Rights Watch February 2009)

(*Observations in her book *Child-Widows Silenced and Unheard: Human Rights Sufferers in Tanzania* by Dr. Monica Elias Magoke-Mhoja, an advocate of the High Court of Tanzania, reinforce the demand made by the Loomba Foundation on the UN to tackle the problems of widows as a human rights issue.)

Dr. Magoke-Mhoja's study brings out vividly the inequality and inconceivable agony child widows, who if they do not die of AIDS, have to endure for long years. She studies the circumstances under which a young girl encounters early marriage and is then widowed under a plural legal system. Most invaluable is her examination of legal pluralism in Tanzania along with an analysis of the interplay between the law and the life that child-wives and child-widows are forced to lead.

She says that child-widowhood is one of the worst repercussions of child marriage. Most importantly, the book highlights the violations of their human rights. The author says that customary norms have been manipulated in order to deny the widows their rightful inheritance. The outcome is impoverishment, violence and the risk of HIV infection, leading to early death.

Dr. Magoke-Mhoja suggests that customary norms should be mediated through international human rights laws, using the principles of gender equality and non-discrimination.

In *Nigeria,* some of the abuses that infect women and girls with HIV / AIDS are: (1) Risks to women and girls in long-term unions; (2) Discrimination in property and inheritance rights; and, (3) Traditional practices that increase HIV / AIDS risk to women and girls.

A *Kenyan* widow's interview was conducted by the Human Rights Watch (2003) on November 2, 2002, which reinforces the argument for the UN to focus on the state of widows around the world and declare it as a Human Rights issue.

In the interview widow Emily Owino—whose narration highlighted the tragedy many widows face—said that she was coerced into sexual cleansing as part of the tradition called "widow inheritance". Her in-laws, shortly after her husband died, took all of her possessions, including farm equipment, livestock, household goods, and clothing. The in-laws insisted that she be "cleansed", by which they meant forcing her to have sex with a social outcast, a custom in her region, as a condition for staying in her own home.

They paid a herdsman to have sex with Owino, against her will and without a condom. They later took over her farmland. She sought help from the local elder and chief, who did nothing. Her in-laws forced her out of her home and she and her children were homeless until someone offered her a small, leaky shack. No longer able to afford school fees, her children dropped out of school.

Another widow Susan Wagitangu, 53, related her woes, which highlighted the practice of 'grabbing' inheritance from widows. When her parents died, her brothers inherited the family land. "My sister and I didn't inherit. Traditionally, in my culture, once a woman gets married, she does not inherit from her father. The assumption is that once a woman gets married she will be given land where she got married."

However, when Wagitangu's husband died, her brothers-in-law forced her off the homestead and took away her cattle. Wagitangu shifted to a Nairobi slum. "Nairobi has advantages," she said. "If I don't have food, I can scavenge in the garbage dump."

Human Rights Watch concluded that "Women's rights to property are unequal to those of men in Kenya. Their rights to own, inherit, manage, and dispose of property are under constant attack from customs, laws, and individuals including government officials who believe that women cannot be trusted with or do not deserve property."

It also urged the United Nations Commission on Human Rights to continue to adopt resolutions on women's equal ownership, access to, and control over, land and equal rights to own property and to adequate housing; the elimination of violence against women; and the protection of human rights in the context of HIV/AIDS.

Violations of Property Rights

An in-depth study of property rights violations by Human Rights Watch in *Kenya* recounted many stories of women being excluded from inheriting property, evicted from their lands and homes by in-laws, stripped of their possessions, and forced to engage in risky sexual practices in order to keep their property.

Many widows were coerced into the customary practice of "wife inheritance" whereby a widow is taken as a wife by a relative of her late husband, or ritual "cleansing" whereby widows are obliged to have sex (usually unprotected) with a man who is a social outcast.

Legislations Defied

Both Human Rights Watch and the Widows Research Report found that legal and judicial remedies for women and girls have been inadequate or non-existent. Even where sexual violence laws are adequate, the laws are rarely enforced. When women or girls are courageous enough to file complaints, law enforcement officials are rarely trained for sensitive and effective handling of sexual and domestic violence cases.

The application of customary laws that mete out injustice to women goes unchallenged despite most African countries having ratified the Convention on the Elimination of All Forms of Discrimination Against Women (CEDAW), which obliges them to eliminate customary laws and practices that are based on the notion of inferiority of women (or of men) or on stereotypes of women.

The author says that customary norms relating to care for widows were manipulated so that they could be denied their legitimate inheritance. The outcome is impoverishment, violence and the risk of HIV infection, leading to early death.

Dr. Magoke-Mhoja also suggests that customary norms should be mediated through international human rights laws, using the principles of gender equality and non-discrimination.

Other Forms of Human Rights Violations

The recent use of rape as a weapon of war is one of the most horrific gender-based violations of human rights in Africa. Rape is used strategically in these cases to terrorise populations and destabilise the economy.

Women and girls in the Democratic Republic of Congo, Sierra Leone, northern Uganda, and Burundi told Human Rights Watch of unimaginably horrific abuses they suffered in civil conflicts in those countries.

It is estimated that 81 million widows (33 per cent) have been abused. This was based on the statistics prepared by

UNIFEM (2003: 6). It estimated that "globally, one in three women will be raped, beaten, coerced into sex or otherwise abused in her lifetime". (Widows Research Report)

International bodies that can exercise some leverage in these situations have done virtually nothing to push for basic protections that could reduce these abuses and mitigate their worst effects.

Widows Displaced Due to Conflicts

Hundreds of thousands of widows and children displaced due to wars, genocide and regional conflicts need immediate attention. The Internal Displacement Monitoring Centre (IDEMC) has been focusing on them for over 10 years. However, the displaced are so widespread that the UN needs to look into how it might persuade governments to act in concert.

Countries where the number of displaced widows and children is high include Afghanistan, Algeria, Angola, Armenia, Azerbaijan, Bangladesh, Bosnia and Herzegovina, Burundi, Chad, Colombia, Congo, Côte d'Ivoire, Croatia, Cyprus, Iraq, Israel, Kenya, Kosovo, Pakistan and many others.

A sample of alerts in *IDP News Alert,* 19 March 2010, is illustrative of the seriousness of the problem. Nigeria: Unending violence causes further displacement in Jos; Kenya: Government asked to address plight of IDPs; Afghanistan: IDPs returning to Marjah struggle to return to normality; Iraq: Little new displacement but around 2.8 million Iraqis remain internally displaced.

The plight of war widows is best illustrated by the example of one Iraqi woman whose husband was killed by Saddam Hussain's soldiers. She had several children to feed but had no money. She begged for a loan. No one assisted her. Desperate to care for her hungry children, she started shouting, "Do you want to have sex with me so that I can buy flour?" It was only then some took pity and gave her money.

(Al-Ali, 2007:200), Iraqi Widows, incorporated in the Widows Research Report.

In *Sri Lanka,* after 30 years of war between Tamil Tigers and the Government there are reportedly 33,000 widows in Eastern Province alone, many suffering from extreme deprivation.

In the wake of the 20 years of war in *Afghanistan,* 65 per cent of widows in Kabul interviewed for a UNIFEM survey (2006) said they considered suicide as an option. (Widows Research Report)

In *Pakistan,* displaced widows have been struggling to cope with distressing level of privation. In IRIN (January 2010), humanitarian news and analysis which is a project of the UN Office for the Coordination of Humanitarian Affairs, an example is given of Razila Bibi, 70, and other women, who left on their own had been forced to learn how to manage without help from husbands and sons.

IRIN said Razila Bibi was among many women who were displaced in the rural areas of Pakistan's North West Frontier Province (NWFP). Aged 70, she had rarely left her home village near the town of Kabal in the conflict-hit Swat Valley before she was displaced in June 2009. Bibi told IRIN: "Since I was married when I was 16 years, I only cared for the livestock and did household tasks. I knew very little about the outside world. I am learning now, at this age."

There is growing concern about the situation of women who are forced to be on their own. Phillipe Fischard, communications delegate in Peshawar for the International Committee of the Red Cross (ICRC), told IRIN, "We have begun investigating the position of widows in the conflict-hit areas, and getting some statistics about the number."

Traditions in most developing countries have also made things difficult for women from conservative areas such as Swat to live on their own. "I am an educated woman, capable of earning for myself. But it would be considered immoral for me to live independently. Women live either with their parents or their husbands," Uzma Farooq Khan, 25, a teacher from Mingora now based in Peshawar, told IRIN. "This makes it hard for widows to find a safe place for themselves to live in, while most are also illiterate and have no means to earn an income."

Widows in the Western World

In developed countries like the United States, widows with low qualifications face severe insecurity particularly because of the healthcare system. They also often struggle to get well-paid jobs. Sometime they have no choice but to move on to state benefits. (Widows Research Report).

The United States "is of particular interest" to any study of widows' deprivation in developed countries due to its higher than average incidence of the range of deprivations, from infant mortality to functional illiteracy". This was noted by the Widows Research Report, citing OECD (2002; 2005). African-American widows are, in particular, at risk of extreme poverty in the United States.

The First Step Towards Widows' Redemption

Various studies, including the global survey the 'Widows Research Report', show that poverty is the primary cause from which stem most other types of woes that deprive widows of their human rights and the freedom to live the way they wish to. The causes of poverty are also manifold: sudden, often complete loss of income owing to the death of a husband, greed of the immediate family, and customary laws that deprive widows of their inheritance rights and displacements.

Poverty prevents widows from taking legal help, even when they know that there are laws to help them. It is an impediment to their ability to fight against avaricious family members and their capacity to live independently and lead a life of dignity. It also inhibits them from acquiring an education or mastering a vocation. It forces them to be dependent on others, who generally exploit their helplessness.

Wars, genocides and HIV/AIDS, malnourishment, and lack of medical facilities are some other causes that lead to early deaths, mostly of men, who leave behind their widows and young children at the mercy of others. Such widows are usually poverty-stricken and are either incapable of working or are forced by the family or the community to be 'inherited', and worse, evicted and abandoned.

Poverty also frequently contributes to high premature male mortality (and therefore, widowhood), through hazardous work—which is most often exploitative. This, was a conclusion drawn by the Widows Research Report.

Analysing Poverty

The Widows Research Report observed that: "While large-scale incidents of poverty are concentrated in certain parts of the world, poverty remains a potent issue that has still not been satisfactorily dealt with in regions that wear the label of advanced countries."

"In all regions, part of poverty's persistence is due to overlooked policy areas, which ultimately stem from overlooked problems, of which widows form an important constituency."

Summation

To reiterate, the UN and its agencies must focus exclusively on the poverty that haunts widows. It should do so separately from the existing measures for poverty alleviation. This issue calls for an immediate policy change and for action for the empowerment of widows.

4

AT A GLANCE: THE STATE OF WIDOWS IN DEVELOPING COUNTRIES

The most oppressed, violated and invisible...

—VANESSA VON STRUENSEE

Africa

The widows in Africa, subjected to varying cultures and customary laws across various regions and states, have endured humiliating and deplorable treatment. Apathy towards their misery worsened their situation. They are, as Vanessa von Struensee, JD, MPH, put it "the most oppressed, violated and invisible and their voices are the most unheard.

"Millions of widows are young mothers, some still children, all subject to extreme discriminatory practices and victims of neglect by governments. The gross human rights violations they experience in many areas of their lives have implications for the whole of society and development in general which cannot be ignored." Such violations include physical, mental and sexual violence, including rape.

The catastrophe that hits them the moment their husbands die is much worse than the misfortune widows face in most other developing countries. Struensee's description of these unfortunate women is distressing. "Their poverty, often due to lack of inheritance and land rights or social support systems, aggravates their vulnerability to violence. The huge increases in the numbers of widows due to AIDS, armed conflict and ethnic cleansing, has resulted in many millions of children being withdrawn from school because of destitution. The vulnerability of widows' daughters and child widows is especially severe, forcing them into unsuitable early marriage and early widowhood, life on the streets, prostitution and other high risk activities such as servile domestic service in the context of trafficking and HIV/AIDS infection."

She indicted governments of doing little to ensure that widows obtained their human rights to inheritance and land ownership. She blames the authorities of ignoring the issue of protection of widows from "gross mental, physical and sexual abuse perpetrated, for example, through coercive traditional practices such as degrading and life-threatening mourning rites; or resulting from cruel accusations of witchcraft leading to their brutal murder. Across cultures widows are 'chased off' from their homes, robbed of their property and have no access to justice systems because these violations occur within the private sphere of the family."

Many instances of widows being subjected to such cruel practices and criminal acts committed against them have been cited in this book. Many of the abuses, like throwing them out of the family, robbing them of their inheritance and declaring them witches, have been and are still being suffered by widows in most developing countries.

There has to be an awareness of the fact that despite anti-discrimination legislations and other measures by most African governments, widows not only fail to take recourse to them because of poverty—75 per cent of the population in Zambia live below the poverty line, 72 per cent in Mali, and 70 per cent in Niger—but also continue to be tormented by customs and culture that have been outlawed. NGOs, despite making commendable efforts, are unable to help on a wide enough scale, though many organisations have helped many widows to learn skills or join cooperatives, which give them independence, and enough resources to be able to take care of their children. But their number is like a drop in an ocean.

The United States Congress recognised the plight of African widows and admitted that discrimination destroyed women's ability to live a life outside of poverty. "In the face of the suffering and injustice widows endure throughout Africa, there is no consensus on the importance of changing the customary legal rules relating to widows, and on the larger question of the proper place of customary law in the changing African society." (*Widows, AIDS, Health and Human Rights in Africa,* Vanessa von Struensee)

Instances cited in other chapters have exemplified how the male members of the widows' families dominate and dictate their lives. The practice of ritual cleansing has led to a high rate of HIV/AIDS infection. In research on widows and HIV/AIDS in Tanzania presented at the 14th International Conference on AIDS, Barcelona, Spain, July 2002, underlines the crisis in Africa.

"The dilemma, torture, stigmatisation and discrimination of HIV/AIDS+ widows from their husband's parents start after their husband's death. Over 60 per cent of widows in Tanzania are HIV+. Often, they do not know their status, although sometimes their husband's parents know this as they get early death certificates written.

"DESCRIPTION: We know HIV+ women are not supposed

to be pregnant. The same to this HIV+ widows others don't have children (sic). So their husband's parents throw them out of husband's property. On top of that they make torture, stigmatisation and discrimination to them. They delay to give their right to inherit (according to inheritance law) as they are waiting for widow's death day. Many widows die before getting their inheritance.

"LESSON LEARNED: In Tanzania, people believe that if partner died of AIDS the rest (husband/wife) will not live for more than 5 years from that time. I'm PLWHA. My husband passed away on April 1997. His parents threw me out of his property and they delay to give me my right to inherit (1/8 of his property according to the Islamic law because I don't have a child). I need treatment, to eat well and to rest in order to live longer. Nobody is taking care of me.

"I can't rest because I am fighting to get my inherit before my death. I can't get proper treatment, eat well as I don't have enough money. I stopped my other activities because my husband's parents taken my works equipments. For 6 years now I am waiting for court's judgment."

Apart from the HIV/AIDS crisis, in many countries like Tanzania and Uganda, reports of discrimination filter through regularly. Discriminatory inheritance laws continue to be effective. The situation has become more complex because of the co-existence of customary, statutory and Islamic laws. Various scholars have cited numerous cases of Tanzanian widows and their children being rendered homeless.

The widows, who refuse or resist customary laws and rituals, are often excommunicated, resulting in their being driven out of settlements. This causes inhuman misery to them and their children. Struensee has cited the case of a widow who refused to fulfil all the burial requirements. She was warned not to return to the village.

Cases of land grabbing, stealing of properties or forcing widows to part with their rightful ownership of property are as common in African countries as in many other developing countries. The authorities have been reluctant to take action against those who "grab" property. The practice of getting widows remarried within the family to keep inheritance is also very common, throughout sub-Saharan Africa.

Many writers have also pointed out that the customary laws and rites are perpetuated by women themselves, with sisters, daughters and aunts upholding such practices. In turn, they too suffer under the same rites and cultural mores. A commentator was quoted on the experiences of widows in Nigeria. Among various reasons cited as to why women support traditional practices harmful to them were "belief in the cultural and social significance of the practice; ignorance of other possibilities; superstition; lack of choice; sense of duty to the family and community; and even love for their husbands."

The only way to change such conceptions and beliefs is to educate, to try to make communities think logically and rationally. This has to be undertaken seriously by Governments which can, in fact must cooperate with NGOs and organisations working for the welfare of widows. Such organisations are active in almost all African states and are ready to help even more so than already are. "A step toward gender equality would begin with a recognition of the autonomy and independence of women and a re-examination of the rationales for the various widowhood practices in the light of changing economic, social, and political circumstances. The solution must include an abolition of those practices considered inhuman and degrading burial rituals, and a recognition of the rights of widows to inherit those properties falling outside the class of family property." (von Struensee)

In the last few years many organisations like the Prince's Trust, Oxfam and the Loomba Foundation have been active in various states to help widows. They have helped create an awareness of human rights, albeit to a limited extent, and have made some realise that customary rules and practices are illegal and immoral. This has encouraged activists and NGOs to persuade some widows to take recourse to legal actions.

Many women's groups are also very active and effective. They have formed cooperatives and provided homes and arranged skills training which has encouraged widows to take their help and escape the customs and lead independent lives. These are wonderful and praiseworthy developments. Women have gradually seen that they can help themselves when no other help is on offer.

However, the struggle still is arduous and long. A majority of African widows remain disadvantaged. The quote in the von Struensee book is relevant. "The minefield task of reforming ingrained customary laws and practices is not one that African women activists can undertake alone."

An absolute accord on customary laws persists. In the interiors there is stiff resistance to efforts of activists. However, in recent years some governments, such as in Ghana and Rwanda, are whole-heartedly helping the likes of Loomba Foundation and Oxfam in helping widows. A joint effort by all of the state governments in close collaboration with the Trusts that are already active in Africa is the only solution. There is also now the African Commission on Human and People's Rights (ACHPR), which is part of the African human rights regime. It is embodied in the jurisprudence of the African Charter on Human and People's Rights (the Charter).

The task has to be undertaken with a sense of urgency and sincerity. If not, mortality and suffering will only increase. Genocide, conflicts and HIV/AIDS have played havoc on the lives of widows and their children. According to UNAIDS about half of all people living with HIV are women. In Botswana 24 per cent of the population suffers from HIV/AIDS while in Lesotho the prevalence rate is 23 per cent. In Namibia it is 20 per cent, Zimbabwe 20 per cent and 19 per cent of the South African population is infected with the virus. In 2005, almost 320,000 people died of AIDS in South Africa while 180,000 in Zimbabwe, 220,000 in Nigeria, 140,000 in Mozambique and 91,000 people in Uganda succumbed to the disease.

Gender inequality puts women at a much higher risk of HIV infection than men and it persists despite states being bound by the principles of the UN Charter, the Universal Declaration of Human Rights, the Convention on the Elimination of All Forms of Discrimination against Women, the Convention on the Rights of the Child, and regional instruments.

Suggestions to 'rescue' widows, apart from laws—which have been largely ineffectual—include extensive educational programmes, while using the NGOs and activists to create awareness in widows of their rights. In fact, in some regions mediators have set up volunteer groups to advise new widows on how to escape customary practices and save homes and belongings.

The last word on the subject was said by Mary Okioma in *Bride Price: Paving the Way for a Killer*, "Thus the plight of African widows needs to be placed on the world stage with the United Nations declaring 23rd June as International Widows Day."

SOME SUGGESTIONS

Hilda Orimba, who attended the International Day of Widows hosted by the Loomba Foundation in London, made some useful suggestions for widows' welfare that can be adopted by all African countries. The national executive chairman of WOWESOK, an organisation helping poor widows to survive, had herself seen what miseries widowhood brings upon women.

The sixth born in a family of eight, she was brought up by a widowed mother. As they mourned the death of their father, a pastor who was a close friend, took their land and divided it among his seven sons. Her mother decided to follow the legal channels to have what was rightfully hers returned. The pastor in turn hired thugs to beat her up and she later died. Hilda would like to work closely in many areas with the likes of the Loomba Foundation. One of the areas she enumerated was education. "The girl-child's education is an epitome [*sic*] of the whole society. We need to focus on education of the disadvantaged. We serve the bottom of the pyramid and therefore the sound upbringing of the girl-child, boy-child, is our cause. In Kenya alone, I have 6,000 orphans currently not going to school due to lack of fees and extreme poverty.

"Although in Kenya there is free primary education not everyone is a beneficiary. We need civic education for widows who happen to be the highest voters in the Republic. Our youth orphans are being used for all manners of crimes political and non-political."

Secondly, she would like increasing advocacy awareness to help upgrade the protection of widows and help them access clean water infrastructure, healthcare, education etc. "We equally need an expanded response to micro enterprise."

She invites cooperation in dealing with HIV/AIDS and collaboration for capacity building, economic empowerment of widows, counselling, gender and governance and advocacy both at policy level and regional levels.

Organisations like hers need to collaborate in terms of investment. "My organisation needs empowerment to address the following gaps; litigation, alterative conflict resolution, issues of globalisation and MDGs, civic education of voters, human rights issues, street children rehabilitation and for breaking cultural barriers that impede social cohesion and development.

"We were given a mandate by the Government of Kenya to develop the tools for monitoring and gendering. Unfortunately, we never received any funding."

These areas if taken up and funded by state governments and aided by the UN would go a long way in restoring human rights to widows of Africa.

Pakistan

A woman becomes a widow, she feels as if the protective chadar from her head has been removed and the status of dependence has been thrust upon her...

Dr. Masuma Hasan, former Cabinet Secretary to the Government of Pakistan and Ambassador, describing their condition in her country said, "Being a widow is not a stigma in Pakistan either in religion or under the law. Marriage in Islam, which is the religion followed by the majority of the population, is not considered as sacrosanct. It is viewed as a civil contract between two individuals which can be dissolved."

Now a member of the Board of Governors of Aurat Foundation in Pakistan, she further explained: "Thus the extreme sanctity attached to marriage in certain other religions does not operate to turn a widow into an outcast or be held responsible for her husband's death."

"Traditionally, widows have been encouraged to re-marry and marriage to a widow has always been considered as an honourable act." There were 2,740,259 widows in Pakistan in the female population of 63,478,593 (as compared to 1,206,305 widowers in the male population of 68,873,686) as per 1998 census. The largest number of 442,179 was found in the age bracket of 75 years and above, followed by 416,773 in age group of 60 to 64 years, and 326,176 between 50 to 54 years. This affirms what Dr. Hasan said. Young widows do tend to get remarried.

The other relatively positive aspect is that the 1973 Constitution and all previous constitutions, do not discriminate between the rights of women and men. "The Constitution guarantees equal rights to both and rules out discrimination on the basis of sex. It empowers the State to make special laws for the protection of women and children.

It stipulates that steps shall be taken to ensure the full participation of women in all spheres of national life and protect the marriage, the family, the mother and the child," said Dr. Hasan.

Widows inherit quarter of their husband's property if they have no children and one-eighth of his property if they have children. The Government has, furthermore, made humane provisions for the widows of its employees. After the death of a Government employee, it is his widow who receives the family pension until her own death. This has been the practice in India too, but there have been cases, particularly in lower middle class families, of other members, even sons and daughters, forcing the widow to hand over here pension.

Dr. Hasan is unsure about private companies. She said, "In the private sector, which works for profit, there are no universal rules governing support for widows of deceased employees, but given the culture of philanthropy, some short-term provision is probably made."

Since 1980, an officially administered *zakat* system has been operating in Pakistan. *Zakat* is levied on Muslims at the rate of 2.5 per cent on 11 categories of assets. (According to some reports *zakat* money in Pakistan is often "captured" by those who are not widows, that is, there is corruption). These funds are used for the benefit of widows, orphans and other needy persons and for those rendered homeless by natural calamities. They are collected by the State and their disbursement has been made the responsibility of the provinces through the provincial *zakat* committees. These committees operate down to the community level and disburse *guzara* (sustenance) allowance, of which widows are also beneficiaries.

Pakistan Baitul Mal (State Treasury), established in 1992, provides financial assistance to widows, orphans, destitutes and invalids, and for welfare projects including education and health care and self-employment schemes. The Government has issued special saving certificates for widows, pensioners and senior citizens. It has also set up First Women Bank and Khushali Bank which operate micro-credit schemes, and many of whose clients are women.

Dr. Hasan said that Pakistan had one of the highest levels of private social investment (philanthropy) in the world, far larger comparatively than rich nations. An initial survey, published in 1999, found that 70 billion rupees were privately donated which was five times more than what Pakistan received in outright grants and larger than the Government's expenditure in certain social sectors. It is an admirable social custom.

"Recently, it has been estimated that 100-120 billion rupees are donated privately every year for welfare, which amounts to 2 per cent of Pakistan's GDP. This sum far outstrips the collection made by the Government as *zakat* (4.67 billion rupees in 2004-5) and is remarkable because Pakistan is a poor country. The volunteering rate in Pakistan is twice that of the global average. Traditionally, supporting widows and orphans, who are the beneficiaries of this philanthropy, has been viewed as acts of piety."

Despite these commendable provisions there are significant regional and class disparities in the status of women in Pakistan that impact on the condition of widows. It is true, however, that in the last two to three decades, women have made a marked appearance on the economic and political scene. One indication of some self-reliance among them, including widows, is the growing number of women-headed households. Studies place the number of such households at one-fifth throughout the world.

An FAO survey of 17 countries in the Near-East in the agriculture sector, as early as 1995, found that women headed households were the highest in Pakistan at 25 per cent (Women, Agriculture and Rural Development in the Near-East: Findings of an FAO Study 1995). In urban areas, women-headed households have multiplied because of the expanding informal sector in which the majority of women work and contribute.

Moreover, urbanisation and increasing female education have given more opportunities to single woman, including widows, to survive and find livelihoods. Urbanisation has also broken many barriers. According to the Pakistan Economic Survey 2004-05, the country has an urban population of over 34 per cent, but unofficial estimates, based on other premises and development indicators, place this figure at well over 40 per cent. The overall female literacy rate (10 years and above) in the 1998 Census was 32 per cent.

However, there were large differences in female literacy between the urban (55.2 per cent) and rural (20.1 per cent) areas. In a big city like Karachi (now14 million inhabitants) there was not much difference between female (71 per cent) and male (76 per cent) literacy rates, between the ages of 15 and 24. On the other hand, there are immense regional disparities in female literacy and access to education opportunities. However, female enrolment at all levels of education is the fastest growing development indicator.

Negative factors

Turning to the negative factors Dr. Hasan said that despite the positive elements in the legal and constitutional parameters, "widowhood is a condition of extreme distress for the majority of widows in Pakistan. To use a local metaphor, when a woman becomes a widow, she feels as if the protective *chadar* from her head has been removed and the status of dependence has been thrust upon her."

Most of the problems of survival that widows face are linked to poverty and two-thirds of the poor live in the rural areas. Poor women, who do not possess land and productive assets, live out the rest of their lives on the fringes of existence. Those who do possess assets can be exploited by the strong male culture, especially in the rural areas. They are also the victims of social and cultural prejudice and abuse.

No government has focused properly on the problems of widows and no specific policy initiatives have been taken to ameliorate their conditions. Dr. Hasan reiterates that the concern for widows falls within the context of concerns about women in general. And as has been repeatedly pointed out at different places in this book the same mistake the UN and its agencies have made. Several measures to help women have failed to help widows because either they are treated as outcasts or are deprived of their rightful share by their families and prevalence of customary laws.

"Legislation discriminatory to women, introduced in the 1980s, has strengthened the hands of conservative forces and eroded the atmosphere of tolerance. Women's and citizens' rights activists, as well as professional organisations, have campaigned forcefully for the repeal of these laws," said Dr. Hasan.

She rightly points out—as also found in the survey conducted for the Widows Research Report—the ability of widows to survive independently and seek livelihoods depends on the level of social and economic development in the region where they live, although there are always some trailblazers. Education brings confidence, but perhaps the most important element is the availability of safe and affordable transport to facilitate the widow's journey out of the protection of her home.

Single women, including widows, take charge of their families and dependants because of male migration, divorce, desertion, and the deaths of husbands caused by war, calamities and natural causes. However, those who do not own land and productive assets may not have access to credit facilities either or possess the skills to earn their own livelihoods.

Many community-based organisations have long realised that women need very small amounts as loans, not tied to collateral, in order to start survival enterprises. Scores of such organisations now provide these small amounts. Poverty still prevents the poorest of the poor from accessing the facilities available in formal institutions like First Women Bank and Khushali Bank.

Kofi Annan, then Secretary-General, United Nations, attending the launch of the International Widows Day in New York in 2005.
Seen in the photo are Raj Loomba, Cherie Blair and Veena Loomba.

Leader of the House of Lords, Baroness Amos, speaking at the International Widows Conference held by The Loomba Foundation at the Foreign and Commonwealth Office in London, on 23 June 2006, the second International Widows Day.

A shanty town outside Nairobi where the Loomba Foundation in partnership with Prince's Youth Business International has set up businesses to empower a number of young widows and their children.

The President of Rwanda , HE Paul Kegame, launches the Loomba Partnership Project in association with OXFAM (GB) and the Rwandan Government to empower 850 widows, including 500 genocide victims, in Kigali in 2009.

Raj Loomba speaking at the UN,
urging official recognition for
June 23 as International Widows Day.

Lord Dholakia, Cherie Blair and Raj Loomba
at Parliament House in London at the launch of
International Widows Day in 2005.

Raj Loomba meeting the UN Secretary General, Ban Ki Moon,
at the United Nations in New York in 2008.

Sir Richard Branson, Loomba Foundation's Patron-in-Chief, seen with HIV orphans supported in South Africa through a community-based partnership project between The Loomba Foundation and Virgin Unite.

Women, including widows, do not get fair remuneration as wages either, although women's rights organisations have lobbied for the reflection of their work in the formal workforce. In the rural areas, they spend long hours in crop and livestock production and in post-harvest activities. However, their control over access to land, labour, agricultural inputs and technology and support services such as credit, extension, training and markets is limited. In the urban areas, due to lack of mobility and access to markets, they are paid far less than their counterpart male workers.

Although assessments of the scale of philanthropy in Pakistan have taken everyone by surprise, the disbursement and use of the large sums generated is random and uncoordinated. Most of it is made in the form of private transfers between individuals. With some initiative and sense of purpose, utilisation of part of the huge amounts donated annually can be accorded priorities and channelised formally into specific programmes for the empowerment of widows.

Lessons from 2005 Earthquake

No single event has thrown up the problems of widowhood in Pakistan quite as dramatically as the earthquake of October 8, 2005. The earthquake measured 7.6 on the Richter scale and the damage it caused was catastrophic. Official estimates placed the number of dead at 79,000, but unofficial mortality figures were as high as 300,000. Most of the casualties were women and children. Half a million children are said to have been orphaned and thousands disabled. It was estimated by the media that 66,000 women became widows and four million people lost their homes. Some women lost not only their husbands but also all their children, their land, homes and livelihoods.

Many widows who were displaced because they had to leave their villages were unable to claim either the compensation paid by the Government to replace their destroyed homes, or the death and injury benefits. Perhaps the greatest upheaval caused by the earthquake was the breakdown of established social support systems and relationships.

Widows who have been absorbed by extended families are generally protected but those living alone now face new and unknown challenges. Security has become the major problem in their lives.

Except by a few NGOs on a limited scale, the rehabilitation and reconstruction strategies adopted after the earthquake have largely not been women or widows-specific, nor have they been designed to address their particular daily needs.

The Aurat Foundation worked in six districts struck by the earthquake, four in the North West Frontier Province (Battagram, Mansehra, Kohistan, Shangla) and two in Azad Kashmir (Bagh and Muzaffarabad). "We were the first to package and distribute female hygiene kits but our effort was a drop in the ocean. In the housing units we are helping to set up on a small scale, as well as in the distribution of food, tents and family survival kits, widows and single women were given priority. We also successfully lobbied that separate desks should be set up by various agencies to address the needs of women. We have started income generation schemes for women in the worst hit areas and are establishing an industrial home in Bakot which will be run by the women of the community," said Dr. Hasan.

Dr. Hasan's explicit description of the state of widows in Pakistan, where despite the fact that they are much better placed in the society than in African countries or in other parts of South Asia, reaffirms the need of the United Nations to take up the cause of widows across the globe. That is well within its power and remit: It must make all of its member-countries focus on their plight and problems by officially adopting June 23 as International Widows Day.

Aurat Foundation's initiative

The Aurat Foundation has established HomeNet Pakistan,

as part of the South Asian network, to build the capacity of home-based women workers, which will also benefit widows. It aims to provide these women, who work from the home, with access to markets and opportunities to network among themselves so that, in time, they should set up their own organisations to strengthen their bargaining power and increase their outreach to resources and assets. Many of these women are widows or single women heads of households.

In consultation with its partner organisations, Aurat Foundation has identified more than 650,000 women in groups for HomeNet Pakistan all over the country. However, it lacks the resources to develop a database. If funds could be made available for this endeavour, we could collect statistics on widows through access to this population, develop a database and conduct a simple survey to identify their actual problems. Only then would it be possible to design reality-based programmes for widows' rights and livelihoods. This will be a beginning for organised work among the widows in Pakistan so that they should not exist on erratic doles but take control of their lives.

(*The Pakistan report is based on Dr Masuma Hasan's report sent to Loomba Foundation for the International Widows Day in June 2006.*)

Bangladesh

Oppression of widows is an extreme form of women's oppression. Women account for the majority of the poor, and widows are the poorest of women...

—WIDOWS WITHOUT RIGHTS

In Bangladesh the status of widows in the family, community and society at large is that of destitution, oppression and marginalisation. Widows face legal, religious, customary and traditional constraints, including barriers to inheritance, land ownership and land use, rules concerning remarriage, and degrading of harmful mourning rites. Not only is their access to basic needs highly constrained, but also the source of livelihood for this unfortunate group is extremely limited.

The elderly widows who form the largest demographic, are unacceptable to the employers because of their age. More often than not, even their close relations refuse to provide them with food or shelter. Abandoned by all, these lonely helpless widows are thrown into the poverty trap and are forced to become heads of their own households.

A very high proportion of widows head the women-headed households. They are among the most oppressed of all women, often without the basic human rights to shelter, food, clothing, dignity, access to services, and denied full participation in social and community life. Their poverty, isolation, dependency, powerlessness and destitution have also harsh consequences for their dependants, the community and for society as a whole.

The status of widows and their families must be seen not merely as a women's issue but as a developmental one. It is often assumed that widows are old women, or that widows remarry, or that they are looked after by the extended family. However, with the poverty situation in Bangladesh, none of these assumptions is valid.

There are hundreds of young and very young widows, even child widows. In some religious groups, widows are debarred from remarriage, while in others they face social criticism from the community they live in. Sometimes they are unwilling to remarry because of anticipated abuse and violence against their children, and because of fear of exploitation and oppression. The extended family is increasingly less likely to be able or willing to support impoverished relatives; on the contrary, many work to evict the widow from her home and grab whatever little property she has after the death of her husband (Shamim, I. & Salahuddin. K., 1995).

The social status and position of widows in Bangladesh are strongly influenced by a set of practices that governs gender relations as a whole. As such, widows cannot be seen in isolation. Property rights and inheritance, remarriage, social support and restrictions that they experience are some of the issues that mould and restrict their lives.

Widowhood and the helplessness that is often associated with it have had severe implications on the livelihood, health and social status of women and their families. Impoverishment and vulnerability of widows (that is 60 years and above, who constituted about the largest category among the widowed population) appear to be the single greatest motivational force for women's oft-stated preference of having a son. In Bangladeshi society, surviving sons are seen practically the only source of social and economic support for their mothers, once they are widowed in old age.

However, the children of widows are more likely to be particularly exposed to ill-health, not only because of economic deprivation (caused by widowhood), but also because a widow often has no choice but to turn to her children as a source of economic support. This has devastating effects, not least because of loss of recreation and leisure, withdrawal from schooling, and exposure to health hazards due to particularly gruelling work.

Rahman (1990) compared the economic decline of widows and widowers in rural Bangladesh and found a much greater decline in the economic status of widows compared to widowers. The reason, he argued, was that for women access to resources was much more dependent on marital status and living arrangements than that of men.

Harrison (1993 articles on Bangladeshi widows cited by many writers) observed that in a traditional society like Bangladesh with the high rates of mortality, many women were left premature widows, and came up with a figure as high as three million for Bangladesh, against only 415,000 widowers. Unable to work outside the home, and with little hope of remarriage, the divorced or widowed women were in an extremely precarious economic situation. In the cut-throat struggle for survival, widows were quite likely to be robbed or cheated of their land if they had any in the first place. The only hope for security for widows was to have as many sons as possible, as they would work on the land for her, and defend her.

Harrison therefore concluded that in Bangladesh—according to surveys—women's ideal family size was significantly larger than that of men. As such he concluded that their low socio-economic status would have to be substantially improved if their fertility—at present their only road to status and security—had to be reduced.

Salahuddin and Shamim (1992), in their study on women in urban informal sector of four slums in Dhaka city, found that widows were the most disadvantaged group. One of the case studies revealed the situation of a young widow, Rashida, aged 35, who was a child bride and migrated along with her landless husband to Dhaka in search of a sustainable livelihood. She became a widow when she was 32 years old with three dependent children to look after. The eldest son took to rickshaw pulling and she started to manage a small business from which she earned a meagre Taka 750 a month, for which she had to work as late as nine in the evening.

Shamim's (1993) study on riverine erosion and coping mechanisms for rural women as managers of households, conceptualised women as principal disaster managers in their productive and reproductive roles. The study was conducted among displaced population living on the embankment of the village Horindhara which is situated in the eastern bank of the Jamuna river in Jamalpur district. Widowed women comprised a large proportion of 66 per cent among female heads.

They mostly fell in the lower income group, mainly due to disintegration of the core family unit and their loss of male support. Among female-headed households, 16 were single women households, of which seven were widows in their sixties, lived in thatched houses on the embankments and were mostly involved in begging. In addition to begging, three of them were involved in income earning activities—selling of rice *pithas* or cakes, rearing poultry and Food for Work programme. The income ranged between *taka* 150 and 300, which was only bare subsistence for survival.

The two studies on Bangladesh clearly brought out the high vulnerability of particular groups of widows, especially those heading households without an adult male. On the other hand, it gives us very little information about the living conditions of most widows who live as dependents in households headed by adult males.

A few studies on widows that were available revealed that elderly widows did not command the respect or attention they were presumed to enjoy in rural society and that these helpless old women were victims of utter neglect. Worse, they had increasingly become economically insecure.

As family support for elderly people in mostly comes from grown-up sons, the failure of the mother to give birth to a son or failure on the part of the grown-up son to support the widowed mother in her old age was a major source of vulnerability for rural women in this category.

Educational Attainment and Economic Activities

Poverty and illiteracy generally go together. An overwhelming majority of the widows (89 per cent) of the four study villages did not have any access to education whatsoever. Since education widens the horizon of knowledge and strengthens an individual to struggle for survival, lack of it adds to the misery of the widows, particularly of those who had no asset of their own or family support to fall back on and were handicapped by age.

The period just after their husbands' death was a very critical time for most of the women who became widows, as they had to decide where to stay, with whom to stay, whom to depend on, whether to work or not and where.

Widows, whether Muslims or Hindus, carried on with their daily chores roles which, though domestic in nature, helped augment the households' resources. These activities were mainly cooking, fetching water, collecting fuel and taking care of children which were expenditure saving, but widows perceived them as extension of the household chores.

A sizeable number of widows had taken up different kinds of income-generating activities after the death of their husbands. The comparative percentage on income earning activities before and after widowhood showed that such activities of widows had increased to a certain extent after the death of the husband, especially due to financial hardship. Widows were involved in various home-based income-earning activities such as selling poultry, eggs, vegetables and fruits, while others were making *shital pati, kantha* and *sikka,* and some of them did bamboo work. There were few widows working outside their household in activities like domestic work, earthwork, picking red chillies, midwifery and day labour. As such, a large majority were sole decision-makers of how their income was to be spent in household matters.

Social Status of Widows

The status of widows in Bangladeshi society is a scene of discrimination, oppression and marginalisation. The lower status of widows in its culture and religions reflects the lower status of women throughout the life cycle. Early marriage, practice of polygamy, wide age gaps between husband and wife, loss of husband through accident, illness and natural disasters, longer life expectancy of women over men, results in there being far more widows in society than widowers. In addition, whereas widowers remarried, for various reasons, widows were less likely to do so given the prevailing customs and traditions regulating the practice of widow re-marriage.

Widowhood and headship were other areas of concern, as there were differences in the status and role of widows living in male-headed households, compared to those who themselves were heading the households. It clearly indicated that not only women-headed households were at the bottom line, but widow-headed households were worse still. More so, with the break-up of the joint family structure and lack of social and economic security from other close relations, widows faced the double burden of not only being left alone to fend for themselves, but also to take care of dependant children.

Discriminatory Traditional Practices

Widows faced isolation in the domain of social interactions. The pronounced form was widows being stigmatised, as being inauspicious and ostracised or left out from religious and social life of the family and society at large. She felt social isolation and alienation from the community where she used to live and share, leading to psychological and emotional stress, resulting in severe consequences. The rules of purity and pollution, and those of inauspiciousness were the means of maintaining social distance. The widow was socially differentiated by a prescribed behaviour, which she had to follow in order to be acceptable in society.

The death of a woman's husband marks the transition from wife to widow—taking the woman, from a central place in the family to its margins, which adversely affects the widow's life. This passage of a woman from the position of a wife to that of a widow is marked by various rites, which indicate that soon after the death of the husband, the appearance of the widow is distinctly marked off from other women.

There is an immediate transformation of status—from wifehood with maximum activity, to widowhood with minimum activity. Women generally experience certain changes in their diet after the death of their husbands. For most of the widows, quality of food deteriorates markedly.

In some cases, changes that occurred in the food habits were both qualitative and quantitative. Because the widows generally were worse off economically when the financial support from the husband was suddenly gone, forcing them to turn to inexpensive food items or the leftovers of the relatives with whom they lived.

Changes in the Participation in Community Affairs

In the traditional Bangladesh society, widows do not participate in all the rituals of a marriage ceremony. The ritual of *gaye halud* is one such rite. Widows, generally, do not participate in this ritual where the guardians, other relatives and friends put a little turmeric paste on the forehead of the bride and bridegroom. Widows appear to be unwanted on many such occasions.

Government Policy Regarding Widows

The Government legislated to give old age allowance to every 10 poorest of the poor older persons of each ward of all Union Parishads. This programme was launched in the fiscal year 1997-1998. Under this programme, more than four hundred thousand elderly persons receive a regular monthly allowance of Tk.100. In addition, since 1998-99, a new programme was launched to provide similar monthly allowance to about two hundred thousand destitute widows and abandoned wives. Tk.100 is given to the five poorest, distressed and helpless widows and abandoned women of every ward under 461 *thanas* all over Bangladesh.

The ward committees invite applications from distressed women. Interested widows and abandoned women apply through a prescribed form. Ward committees then recommend the names of five widows and abandoned women to the *thana* committee which finalises the list of the aid recipients.

- Priority will be given to the oldest distressed widows and abandoned women.
- Helpless and landless widows and abandoned women who have two children below the age of 16 will get priority.
- Handicapped and sick widows and abandoned women will also get priority.

SANWED's Bangladesh Chapter

In the backdrop of the existing status and rights of widows, the South Asian Network for Empowering Widows in Development (SANWED) Bangladesh Chapter was formed in January 2006 with a view to upholding the rights of widows. It is represented by 12 network NGOs as core members with 30 associate member organisations throughout Bangladesh. The member organisations are involved in micro-financing widows to empower them economically and are running non-formal education for the children of widows in their mainstreaming development programmes.

It works to sensitise and involve the Government departments on the issue of widow's rights effectively and identify what steps have been taken for the interests of the widows. Members would work side by side with Government for proper implementation of the initiatives: Awareness programmes are organised focusing on widow's sufferings, deprivation, violation of the rights, through media coverage, rallies, roundtable meetings, and street drama.

It launched a 'Helpline for Widows' in each district with the assistance of concerned authority.

It also suggests strategies for future action and building a social support system. Direct Government intervention is necessary to protect the quality of life of the widows after the death of the husbands. In the case of the helpless, shelter-less destitute widows a system of direct transfers in cash or kind or both may be introduced, it suggests.

The children of widows face multiple disadvantages and deprivation. They should be given top priority by government and NGOs that are working with children's development issues such as health and education.

It also wants employment opportunities and access to

resources for widows. "Access of widows to remunerative employment opportunities can play an important role in protecting widows from deprivation. Both government and non-government interventions are needed to create employment opportunities for widows.

"Expansion of education, training and health facilities for widows and supply of credit to them may enable widows to earn incomes through self-employment. Widows may be allowed to have special access to public sector wage employment. They may be accorded top priority in the rural works programmes.

Widows should have access to public sector wage employment and formal credit institutions in various rural projects undertaken by government and non-government organisations.

In fact, an important role can be played by NGOs in organising poor widows for self-employment. Many NGOs are engaged in promoting self-employment for women. They may give special attention to poor widows, particularly the rural widows.

Most importantly, a steep change in social attitude is needed so as to erase discrimination against widows. Widows must be organised so that their voices can be heard.

Afghanistan

Kabul has become the capital of widows...

The problem of widows is acute in war-torn Afghanistan. The country has one of the highest number of widows per proportion to its population, as a result of two decades of armed conflicts. They have not only lost their husbands, but most are displaced, homeless and are troubled by loss of identity. According to Beyond 9/11, a US-based non-profit group, they number over two million out of an estimated 26.6 million people in Afghanistan.

No wonder Kabul is called the capital of widows. Around 70,000 of them, quite a number being young, live in the city. Visitors to Kabul can see many widows—mostly in their 30s—with children with them, begging on the streets. It is said that begging is a profession for many, from 7 am to 6 pm. According to IRIN News, January 30, 2008, they earn around 100 to 150 Afghanis ($2.50).

The report cited the case of one Zulaika who lost her husband, Jamaluddin, in factional fighting between former Taliban and Northern Alliance forces in the northern outskirts of Kabul in 1999. She has three children—an 11-year-old son and two daughters aged eight and nine. Over the past three years she has been living in a shack outside Kabul, for which she pays a monthly rent of $15. "We have nobody to help us," the widow said.

That is the tragedy of most widows. Those who are sheltered in camps face the problem of proving their identity. They have lost everything and are illiterate. The Afghan Ministry of Women's Affairs said that food, shelter and protection are the biggest issues for these widows. A UNIFEM Survey (2006) found that 65 per cent of the 50,000 widows in Kabul saw suicide the only option to get rid of their miseries and desolation. *Indo Asian News Service* noted that during winters, when fuel and food costs increase, female-headed households become highly vulnerable.

The Afghan widows are mostly traumatised, having first suffering the shock of the loss of their husbands and then getting displaced, and face rebuilding of their and their children's lives anew, without any money or help. According to reports the UN agencies are trying their best, but there is a total lack of donors. According to IRIN, women's rights activists such as Soraya Subhrang, a member of Afghanistan Independent Human Rights Commission, have criticised the government and international donors for not doing enough to alleviate the plight of widows. "Afghan women in general and widows in particular do not have a voice to express their problems and are also deprived of meaningful representation in public institutions." Ministry of Women's Affairs officials agreed that Afghan widows often live in wretched conditions.

Caroline Moorehead writing in the London-based *Open Democrcay* reiterated that Afghanistan was the land of widows. "The gravest long-term casualties of war in Afghanistan are not the refugees, but the many thousands who were too poor to flee. Among these internally displaced people, women and children are hardest hit." According to the Internal Displacement Monitoring Centre in March 2010 there were around 240,000 conflict-induced IDPs. It noted that internal displacement was again on the rise as a result of the intensification of fighting in many regions. "Displacement is becoming more protracted due to insecurity in the south, southeast, east and west. Data-tracking and the provision of humanitarian aid are inordinately difficult due to security and logistical constraints particularly where displacement serves as a short-term coping mechanism."

Moorehead gave the example of three widowed IDPs. She wrote about Anja, Fatima, and Salima, who came from the same village in the highlands of the Hindu Kush, not far from Bamiyan and its shattered Buddhist statues. "They have known each other for a long time. Anja, who is Fatima's mother-in-law, is in her early 60s, while the two younger women are barely in their 30s. All the three look considerably older. Fatima's face is deeply lined; Salima is very thin and listless.

"All the women are widows, their husbands killed at different times in the fighting between the Mujahideen and the Taliban, when the Taliban came to their valley and laid waste to their homes and fields. Together with nine children under the age of 15, they share two rooms in the old centre of Kabul, in an area of bombed and derelict houses. Around them refugees from other parts of the country, and returnees from exile abroad, perch in squalor and destitution. The smell of faeces and rubbish is overpowering."

The problem, she pointed out, was that the likes of Anja, Fatima and Salima were neither technically refugees nor returnees. "They are internally-displaced people (IDPs in the official language of humanitarian work), made homeless by the years of civil war. Now, as widows with no living male relations to help them, they are among the most destitute people in the new Afghanistan. They were too poor to make the journey into exile during the civil war, and are thus not eligible now for the benefits that have gone and continue to go to the refugees who were able to make it across Afghanistan's borders into Iran and Pakistan during the Soviet (1979-1989), Mujahideen (1989-1996) and Taliban (1996-2001) years."

International help is not forthcoming to even approaching some meaningful extent. The conclusion, rather tragic and troubling, is that Afghanistan has become a country of displacement, "of refugees who have returned after long periods of exile abroad. Many drift from one end of the land to the other, in search of safety or food. It is estimated that half the population no longer lives in the place they once saw as home".

The United Nations High Commission for Refugees (UNHCR), other UN agencies and other foreign NGOs are active locally in great numbers, investing money and human resources into the country. But although these agencies are trying to offer the internally displaced the same help they provide for returnees from abroad, the situation of the IDPs is growing ever more desperate, noted Moorehead.

The religion allows remarriage which could resolve the problems of most, as the majority are young. However, according to Sharmeen Obaid-Chinoy, writing in the *Independent* most Afghan men do not want to bring up children from a previous marriage. There is no social security system in Afghanistan either. Widows are not provided pensions or housing so there is no safety net for them to fall back on. "In other Muslim countries, getting remarried can resolve the economic problems of widows. But in Afghanistan that is not so."

Maria Akrami, quoted by Obaid-Chinoy, said, "War widows often stand outside government buildings holding frayed photographs of their late husbands. They should be the government's top priority. These women are uneducated; they lack basic job skills and cannot fend for themselves. If America invaded us to liberate our women, this is a clear sign that they are failing miserably."

Nepal

Agony and humiliation is attached to the word widow in Nepali...

—LILY THAPA

The situation of widows is pitiful in Nepal. Buffeted between age-old customs and discrimination most of them have to endure humiliation all of their lives. Many activists have been trying to help them, with Lily Thapa, Chairperson of Women for Human Rights, succeeding in getting support from various organisations. However, the problem is the number of widows in Nepal is very large due to the armed conflicts in recent years that cost over 15,000 lives.

Most of the dead in the decade-long conflict that ended in 2006 were in their 20s or early 30s. They left young widows who could not, because of tradition, remarry. While neglected by their husbands' families they have had to fend off sex predators and save themselves from being trafficked, while trying to earn enough for themselves and their children.

"In a patriarchal and male-dominated society like Nepal, where women are systematically discriminated, the status of widowed women (to whom we use the term 'Single Women' due to the agony and humiliation attached in the word widow in Nepali) is totally low and they are the most marginalised and abused sector of the population.

"The scenario worsens no sooner than the Nepalese woman is widowed and is begun to be seen as a curse befallen the family," said Thapa. She added, "They are put through a life of humiliation and are always looked at with hatred and suspicion. The moment they become single they lose their independence and every means of happiness and get tied down by the ancient iron rules, culture, systems and beliefs of the society."

Research by Women for Human Rights showed that nearly 70 per cent of Nepal's widows were young, between 20 to 35 years. While almost 30 per cent widows were illiterate, only 2 per cent had received higher education. Over 10 per cent were displaced due to the conflict.

The high incidence of HIV and other diseases in the country also add to the number of widows. A large number of villages, due to hilly terrains are almost inaccessible and people are generally illiterate. Many widows carry the disease. This adds to their misery.

According to the research, widows in Nepal suffer huge social stigma. They do not wish to get remarried, being apprehensive of ill-treatment by their second husbands. Marriage, in fact, according to the research, was not the priority for widows, but social security payment, ration cards, health care and education for the children were. A recent *Unreported World* documentary Channel 4 in the UK (2009), "Nepal: The Living Dead", vividly documented these aspects of young widows' lives.

A major problem is the ingrained belief that the death of husbands is quite often because of wives bringing ill-luck to their in-laws' families. The widows are called BOKSHI, or witches, and "are subject to extreme abuse and discrimination. This practice continues, evidenced by the death in June 2001 of a woman killed during an attack provoked by those in her village who accused her of witch-craft" revealed the office-bearers of the Witch-Hunting Awareness Program. "The worst problem is that we still don't have any laws to apply harsh punishment to those who torture women in their witch-hunt," said rights activist Samjha Shrestha.

These atrocious acts occur because people believe that these women, once widowed, harbour evil powers to harm themselves and others. These accusations, however, are derived from unfounded superstitions. Many of the victims have led very difficult lives, and once accused of being a 'bokshi', they are beaten, tortured, or forced to commit degrading acts such as eating human waste, or even human flesh.

The Women's Foundation (WF) has been raising awareness about the witch-hunting. The WF activists concentrate their efforts in the regions where there is more belief in widows being 'bokshis'. A series of cassette tapes were also made a few years ago. These tapes recorded the stories and issues faced by Nepali widows, and were distributed widely in the remote areas of Nepal, along with tape players. It was hoped that through education, there would be awareness of what damage this superstitious belief inflicts on widows.

Several measures have been taken by the Nepalese Government but according to the women activists much still needs to be done. They also opposed the Government's plan in 2009 for grant of money for couples of inter-caste, as well as to those who married widows. It planned to provide each inter-caste couple 100,000 Nepali rupees ($1270) to encourage marriage between the so-called lowest Dalit caste and non-Dalit castes and 50,000 Nepali rupees ($635) to each couple when a widow remarries. The couples were to receive such grant within 30 days of marriage registration at district administration.

While the grant offered for inter-caste marriages was welcomed by some caste activists, the widows of Nepal were up in arms about the Government plan. Women for Human Rights, the human rights group with 44,000 registered members from 52 districts (which under its Single Women Group had been working for widows' rights for the past 14 years), officially lodged a protest demanding the government to rethink the policy with petition from the 52 districts. The protesters argued rightly that men would be only financially motivated to marry and widows could be viewed as an opportunity for monetary gain. Payments for remarriage may lead to further discrimination against widows.

What if a husband abandons his wife after getting money? Will remarriage empower widows? Can the meagre sum of money resolve the issues of social stigma of widows? What about the children from the former husband and their future?

Dalits comprise 13 per cent of the population in the country. They are still considered untouchables, although discrimination against them was outlawed in the 1960s. Reports of suicide by inter-caste marriage couples or forced removal of such couples from villages by the villagers frequently appear in the Nepali media. The state of widows in the community is in no way better than that in the upper castes.

The Government pays 500 Nepali rupees (less than $7) to widows over 60 but it is too meagre. The Government also announced sometime ago that it would collect the data of widows to introduce measures to increase widows' access to employment opportunities and to review the allowance facilities in future.

But governmental measures as with elsewhere in the subcontinent have largely failed. The customary laws are still in operation. One person Lily Thapa and her colleagues have been doing work on the ground, but she needs encouragement and support from the UN and other governments. She has been saying that generally, in Nepal, a 'women's position is derived only from her relationship with the men under whose relational or legal protection she is. This is her father, brother, husband and then her son during her later years.

"In a Hindu society, religious and cultural practices have maintained implicit and explicit rules whereby woman has restricted mobility, no decision-making and no access to resources. Poverty, illiteracy and the conflict situation force single women to seek refuge in informal sector and high chances of trafficking have occurred. The situation clearly shows that single women suffer both economically and emotionally. The rising number of young single women resulting from the conflict has forced them to tear away from the cultural and social codes and ethics and face the world with no skills and tools for earning driving them to trafficking and vulnerabilities."

Thapa pointed out that hundreds of widows "are displaced from various districts and working in the informal sector out of dire necessity, such as sex workers, in bars and as maids and helpers for very low pay. Such single women are extremely vulnerable to abuse and torture".

The problem is compounded by the fact that there is no concrete authentic data and information related to single women and no data on single women (widows) who have been displaced to urban areas and pushed into the informal employment sector.

There is, furthermore, still no mechanism to address psychological trauma and mental distress of single women. There are no immediate trauma or relief centres that will assist single women and their children. These are mostly young women. A study on status of widows in Nepal conducted by Women for Human Rights has found 67 per cent of the widows are between 20 to 30 years of age. It also revealed that most of the single women were traumatised and were most vulnerable victims in terms of basic need, health, education and psychological impacts.

Although the constitution of Nepal guarantees equality among all citizens, there are still more discriminatory provisions in various laws against single women that conflict with rights provided under the CEDAW—the UN's Convention on the Elimination of All Forms of Discrimination Against Women convention. Strong patriarchal culture and conservative practices emphasise traditional role of a single women. This is a major hurdle in the implementation of human rights convention in Nepal. "Lack of conceptual clarity related to the women's human rights and to the principle of equality among people has created confusion, which further limits single women's fundamental rights and freedom. Most of the women in rural areas are not fully aware of their human rights as well as not aware of any kind of conventions, declarations that the government has signed in."

The CEDAW committee made some suggestions to the Government in 2004. This has had an effect. A few changes were made in the discriminatory laws, mostly through the Eleventh Amendment to the country code of Nepal, which stated single women's rights to property. The Government took some initiatives to monitor their actual implementation but only for women made widows by conflict. It bypassed other marginalised single women. The Government also started some social security measures to address the needs of single women by providing compensation to the spouse of the deceased, scholarships, services at health posts and identifying the measures through programme planning.

Thapa and others pointed out that a mechanism to make the women's voices heard at all levels was needed. For that to happen there have to be proper provisions to measure the implementation of the CEDAW convention, as well as UNSCR 1325. There is also the need to protect women's rights as detailed under Geneva conventions and CEDAW conventions and to curb increasing violence against single women. Thapa pointed out that the lack of necessary resources to organise the single women in the communities affected the activities that were identified to bring them in the mainstream.

Thapa's Women for Human Rights has been addressing all these issues and mobilising thousands of young single women in 170 village development committees of 40 districts of Nepal since last 14 years. The single women groups in the districts are playing an active role in the peace movement, whose work is met with tremendous support from local level and national level.

The report about the fight by Women for Human Rights for salvaging widows in Nepal from their plight and pain must be reached to all agencies and societies working for the redemption of widows across the developing countries. It would surely encourage them to fight for widows. The example of Thapa would encourage many widows to emulate her.

Thapa lost her husband, a surgeon with the UN, when she was quite young. He had died in the Gulf war. She faced the same situation as all widows in Nepal do. She lost her status, her hair was chopped off, her bangles were broken and the nose pin was removed with a pair of pliers. As Margaret Owen put it in *The Guardian*, "Not only had she to suffer widowhood, she had to be seen to suffer widowhood."

Thapa had however more spirit and determination. She soon began to wear multi-coloured saris (widows in Nepal traditionally wear black for the rest of their lives). She grew her hair. Her defiance proved to be a challenge to the obscurantist vision of widowhood. Thereafter her battle for legislative changes started. Now widows do not have to return all property that belonged to their first husband if they remarry. They do not need a male consent to get a passport or the consent of their adult children if they want to pass on property.

As Owen said, "Widows may not have the rights they are yet entitled to, but they have more rights than they used to have, thanks—at least in part—to Thapa."

The UN and its agencies and other governments have to produce more Thapas if they are sincere in their efforts to restore womanhood to widows.

Sri Lanka

> *If men were the principal casualties of war, these widows (of the North and East) represent its collateral damage...*
>
> —Ed Payne

Peace has been restored in Sri Lanka after over three decades of war between Sri Lankan forces and Tamil rebels. But its tragic legacy is an estimated 35,000 war widows—many say that the figure is much higher. According to USAID report (in 2009) there were more than 25,000 widowed heads of households in northern Sri Lanka's Jaffna district. In Kopai alone, there were 1,300 war widows and nearly 10,000 war-affected family members. Thousands more were displaced from their homes by "high security" zones, and two camps for displaced people remained, rendering Kopai among the poorest parts of the country.

The situation of these widows has been miserable. They not only lost their husbands but also many were displaced from their homes. They are vulnerable to disease, abuse and violence. The Government announced several measures but activist groups have said that authorities did not have any commitment nor did they appear sincere in helping the traumatised widows. These widows, uprooted from their homes, need sympathy and help in rebuilding their lives. They also wish to have their children educated and their health taken care of.

According to the findings of many independent researchers, the issue of widows in Sri Lanka is more complicated, because of their mental trauma which can last for many years. In an article "The Mental Health Issues of Sri Lankan War Widows" Dr. Ruwan M. Jayatunge wrote that "Depressive reactions are common among the Sri Lanka war widows. In 2005, 86 Sri Lankan war widows were clinically interviewed based on Beck's depression scale and depression was diagnosed at 23. Ten war widows said that they had contemplated suicide after they lost their husbands."

Like in other countries in the Indian sub-continent widows in Sri Lanka too are considered bad omens. They are humiliated and marginalised. Dr. Jayatunge found that the war widows, having suffered bereavement as a result of the violent deaths of their husbands, are hounded by traumatic memories for many years. They are often subjected to extreme forms of discrimination and physical, sexual, and mental abuse. Therefore, widowhood represents a form of social death for these women. Their plight and vulnerability lead to numerous psychological ailments.

In the overall view, a large proportion of women display severe psychological damage, including intrusive memories about their dead husbands; fear and uncertainty about the future; self pity; low self-esteem; sleep disturbances; irritability; displacement of anger; emotional numbing; feelings of guilt for being happy; and psycho-physiological reactions such as persistent headaches and backaches. These last ailments are without any medical basis and do not respond to painkillers.

Most often, the complaints involved chronic pain and problems with the digestive system, nervous system, and reproductive system. These young war widows who have suppressed their biological needs following cultural pressure and 'family honour' often manifest conversion reactions.

Professor Rachel Tribe and Padmal De Silva (senior lecturer in psychology at the Institute of Psychiatry, University of London) in their research paper "Psychological Intervention With Displaced Widows" in Sri Lanka highlighted the importance of integrating coping strategies, self-help principles, changing perceptions, attitudes and stereotyped beliefs when improving mental health issues of the Sri Lankan women who were widowed following extreme traumatic events. They recommended that the cultural and socio-political issues should be taken into consideration.

Dr. Jayatunge said the higher levels of stress and mental illness among women, common in many post-conflict societies, "may be even higher in Sri Lanka due to the prolonged war. The war widows carry an extra burden more than the average woman in Sri Lankan society. Apart from their traumatic experience, daily stressors such as poverty, family conflict, health problems, unemployment, social isolation and harassment exert a significant effect on their stress levels. Some widows take care not only of their children but often of their extended family as well."

He suggested that the mental health interventions of the war widows should be followed with the specific cultural contexts and not contradicting religious beliefs of the victims. The war widows need strength-based psychosocial interventions. Welfare and rehabilitation of widows are essential with teaching coping strategies, facilitating education and job training for the socially shunned widows. The measures are needed to help women to transform their new skills into financial independence and sustainability and strengthen women's existing skills and to introduce new skills in traditional and non-traditional fields.

"There must be a permanent rehabilitation policy for the war widows at the national level that helps widows to build a new life, regain confidence and gently adjust to a new life. The children of these war widows should have a secure and dignified future as their fathers always expected. It is the duty of the nation to repay their dues to these families who have become the invisible victims of the Eelam war."

The USAID provided counselling programmes to help widows cope and their children to go back to school. Father Damian, who helped war widows to cope widows with their trauma and persuade their children to go to schools was quoted as saying. "Everybody is very happy with the results—the parents, the school principal, and we at the center, of course. I don't know what the future holds for children if they don't go to school."

With help from USAID, Father Damian Soosaipillai, a Catholic priest and clinical psychologist at the Jaffna teaching hospital, has been running a health centre that has been using counselling to help families traumatised by war and displacement restart their lives. Among its main goals are keeping children from these families in school and getting drop-outs to return.

"Children drop out of school because of poverty, a lack of supplies, poor family environments, and undernourishment," Father Damian said. "Absence of basic reading, writing, and thinking skills perpetuates the cycle of poverty in the district." Initially, dropouts avoided meeting the centre's staff. But weekly gatherings, with a free lunch, began to attract mothers for trauma counselling and up to 100 children at a time. "At group meetings for mothers, we don't address the trauma alone," he said. "We take up issues like education. We try to sensitise them and empower them by explaining that basic education is necessary for their children."

The USAID report said, "Following traumatic events, children are sometimes unable to learn or show clinging or aggressive behaviour, leading to high dropout rates. Since USAID began funding the programme in 2004, about 35 school-age drop-outs, or 20 per cent of the area's estimated drop-outs, have returned to the Sirupddy Government Mix School in Kopai."

However, the number of widows is too large. Widow welfare groups maintain that the counselling has to be taken up at a much larger scale and for a sustained long period. They could be right. Instances reported by BBC showed the state of agony and trauma of most widows. One Jeyarulai Puwanendran, a single mother, 23, related her plight. While weeping, she said, "My husband was a fisherman. About three years ago, when he returned from a fishing trip, somebody checked his identity card and shot him dead." She further told BBC, "I have a four-year-old daughter. I don't get help from the Government or anybody else. My parents are the ones who look after my daughter and me. My father is a labourer. They have six other children apart from me."

Many have narrated such tragic tales. The widowed belong to all of the communities, Sinhalese, Tamil and Muslim. In recent years and particularly after the end of the war, several organisations have begun to help the widows. Most groups have alleged that widows continue to be in agony and suffer. They, however, conceded that the Government was aware of the problems of widows and identified the issues that need to be tackled.

One activist said that there were two underlying hurdles. One, there was lack of adequate funds for implementing relief programmes and, second, that at the ground level, the long years of conflict created so much hatred between the 'needy' and the 'helpers' that sympathy and commitment were woefully lacking.

However, the Government has been maintaining that relief work was being done keeping in view the fact that most widows were under 30. A survey was also undertaken to understand the needs of the widows. A government spokesperson assured that the authorities were committed to helping widows. Plans were readied to provide widows opportunities for self-employment, foreign jobs and jobs in the livestock and agricultural sector. It also said that a huge budget was allotted for development. Many small-scale industries could thus have been started which would give employment to many.

Critics and widows' welfare groups, however, insisted that development in the east was not very satisfactory. Most Tamil, Sinhala and Muslim widows, who had suffered severely due to war, have alleged that they had no official help and were struggling to cope with their miserable situation. And shock and trauma.

5

WIDOWS' REMARRIAGE: A COMMUNITY SHOWS THE WAY

The Vedas, acclaimed as being among the oldest scriptures of the world, contain explicit references to widow remarriage...

Not many people, including sociologists, however, may be aware that there is a community in India which has, for ages, practised institutionalised remarriage of widows. What is more important is that the institution seems to have been carefully designed with elaborate rules and procedures based on the highest degree of human sensitivity, rational human behaviour and the most progressive principles of equity and equality. Equally significant is the fact that being a long-standing convention, it has acquired a great force of moral, social and legal sanction based on complete unanimity on its desirability as well as modality.

Interestingly, this hoary tradition with all its attendant moral force and social sanctity prevails even today in the community. It is also remarkable that the tradition remained unaffected by contrary beliefs and practices among most other communities in India.

The community happens to be that of the Jats, who have been well known, historically, for being equally deft at wielding the sword and the plough. There seems to be a general consensus among historians about the Jats being the earliest community to have graduated to settled agrarianism from a state of nomadic pastoralism. Occupying the best of arable lands, the majority of them have been living in the northern plains of India stretching from Sind to Punjab, Rajasthan, Haryana, western Uttar Pradesh, and parts of Gujarat, Madhya Pradesh and Maharashtra. History also tells us that the community has quite often clashed with and has borne the first brunt of foreign invaders, most of whom attacked India from her northern and northwestern frontiers. Converting barren and forest lands into fertile cultivable ones and frequently facing wars obviously took a heavy toll on human lives, mostly of the males who were the breadwinners of the family. The loss of male lives under such circumstances must have impelled community leaders to devise the system of widow marriage.

The Jats are acknowledged as being among the best warriors of the country. Not surprisingly, they regard themselves as a martial race and therefore descendants of the Aryans. The institution of widow marriage adds weight to the assertion.

Modalities of Remarriage

The ingenuity displayed in the elaborate detailing of the conditions, the timings and the procedures for widow marriage are impressive. Almost nothing has been left to chance or ambiguity. Yet, it is neither rigid nor oppressive. It is quite enlightening to note that a lot of flexibility and freedom has been granted in almost all matters, such as the choice of another husband, concurrence of the widow, and mutual agreement between the parents and the in-laws.

The first condition for remarriage is that the woman concerned should be young and not too old. Second, she must be willing. Third, her parents must approve of the match. Fourth, her having any children from her late husband will not disqualify her in any manner. Most importantly, remarriage does not carry any stigma at all. She is accepted as a good wife by the family and the community at large.

In matters of property and paternity too there is no confusion. The devolution remains paternal in that the sons and daughters would inherit the name and the property of their respective fathers.

The most appropriate time prescribed for solemnising the (re)marriage is the last day of mourning after the death of her husband, which usually is the twelfth (Barahwan) or the thirteenth (Terahvin). However, the choice of the day varies from region to region.

In exceptional cases, especially if the death has been too tragic or the proposed husband is not of the requisite age yet, the wedding may take place on the first death anniversary. The principle being that the sentiment in the family(ies) would be so emotive on such an occasion that the arrangement would be easily accepted by all, including the widow and her in-laws. Importantly, the mourning would ensure the presence of all the near and dear ones as a matter of course.

The most interesting aspect of the system is that the responsibility for the resettlement vests with the in-laws of the widow. Therefore, they take the initiative and make the offer. If they are found dilly-dallying, the community exerts moral pressure on them, first through close relatives, to be followed by the community panchayat.

Preferred Second Husband

The most preferred prospective husband is the younger brother of the deceased. If he is not available or is not of marriageable age at the time, there are other options too. A first cousin within the immediate family of the in-laws or on the maternal side of the deceased could be considered. In exceptional cases even the elder brother of the late husband can marry the widow. An unmarried person of the husband's distant family relatives can also offer himself in marriage. However, in more exceptional circumstances, even a married younger and elder brother can marry. Over the years precedents have become custom. Of course, and importantly, all details and arrangements are sorted out through consultations and *mutual* agreement.

The choice, however, is subject to the concurrence of the widow. Should a widow be emotionally traumatised and does not wish to remarry, she is not pressured and is left to come to terms with her grief in time. If she chooses to remarry at a later stage, the community follows custom. Remarrying is not mandatory and the decision is entirely up to the widow to take.

The other modalities prescribed for remarriage are at once simple and elaborate. The eldest among the future in-laws of the lady offers the hand of the prospective husband to the visiting parents of the widow, privately first. Should the potential groom be acceptable to them, he is presented to them publicly. The most senior member of the widow's family places some token money, generally a rupee, in the hands of the proposed groom. The female relatives of the man then cover the widow's head with an *odhni* or a *chaadar* (shawl) and make her wear bangles again, as the earlier ones were ritually broken following the death of her husband. She then once again wears a *bindi* on the forehead and applies red *sindur* (vermilion) in the parting of her hair. The ritual is consciously kept simple and brief without ostentation. The ceremonies of (re)marriage and mourning are then deemed to have concluded simultaneously.

Divorce is prohibited and as a concept is rather alien to the community. It is interesting to note that there is no equivalent word to 'divorce' in Sanskrit, the most ancient of all languages. The reason being that a wife in ancient Vedic tradition was regarded as *saamraajyin* or 'empress'—she embodied the prestige and pride of the family, something that couldn't have been allowed to be lost under any circumstance. The Jats subscribe to this notion and uphold it with much pride.

It is equally noteworthy that the Jats have never practised the ritual of *sati,* according to which the widow immolates herself on the burning pyre of the deceased husband. *Sati,* along with many other atrocious malpractices, is supposed to have been institutionalised in Hindu society during the medieval period in India. Some communities eulogised this ghastly ritual as one of the most pious religious duties of Hindu women. The Jats have never subscribed to the idea.

Vedic Mantras

The ancient Vedic civilisation too had no such custom. Rather, the Vedas, acclaimed as the oldest scriptures of the world, contain explicit references to widow marriage. Rig Veda, the first of the four Vedas, contains the following *mantra*:

Udirshva naaryabhi jivalokam gataasumetamupa shesha ehi,

Hastagraabhasya didhishostavedam patyurjanitvamabhi sambabhuvah... (Rig.10/18/8)

Addressing the widowed woman, the mantra exhorts her to rise and look to the living world, and let the deceased go away. It also asks her to consummate a relationship with another man willing to hold her hand and obtain potent energy in order to procreate.

Rig Veda (10/10) also permits a woman whose husband is incapable of procreation to remarry. It says thus:

Anyamichhasva subhage patim mat...

Another Rig Veda mantra (10/85/40) identifies four types of husbands:

Somah prathamo vivide gandharvo vivida uttarah
Tritiyo agnishte patisturiyaste manushyajah...

The first type is known as 'somah' and the second 'gandharvah', and the third 'agnishte'. These three are regarded as the superior ones. The fourth type is 'manushyajah' or the ordinary one.

It is clear that women in early Vedic times could generally marry several times. The following *mantra* (Rig.8/3/28/5) suggests up to 11 marriages:

Imaam twamindra meedhwa suputraam subhagaam krinu
Dashaasyaam putraanaam dhehi patimekaadasham kridhi...

A *mantra* in Atharva Veda (18/3/1/1) asks men to deem it as a religious duty to provide semen to a woman whose husband has died to help her procreate:

Iyam naari patilokam vrinaanaa nipadyata upa twaa maryyam pretamo
Dharma puraanamanupalayanti tasyai prajjam dravinam cheh dhehi...

The *Nirukta,* the most authentic dictionary-cum-thesaurus of Sanskrit, which details the nuances and contextual meanings of important Sanskrit words, contains the following:

Devarah kasmaad dwiteeyo varo uchyate... (3/15)

Even the much maligned and misunderstood Maharshi Manu permits the widow to remarry. He says:

Taamanena vidhaanena nijo vindeta devarah... (Manusmriti 9/69)

Manu also lays down in 9/59:

Devaraadvaa sapindaadvaa striya samyang niyuktaya,
*Prajepsitaadhigantavyaa santa***a***nasya parikshaye...*

The widow can remarry within the same family or go with some other man, if she desires to have children. Manu's liberalism goes even further in 9/76 when he permits a woman to remarry in any of the following circumstances:

Proshito dharmakaaryaartham prateekshyoashtau narah samaah Vidyaartham shad yashoartham vaa kaamaartham treenstu vatsaraan...

That is, if the husband is away on religious work, she should remarry after waiting for eight years; if for education, after six years; if for business, or fame, then only after three years.

In modern times, it was Swami Dayananda Saraswati, the founder of Arya Samaj, who in addition to initiating several social reforms, campaigned for remarriage of widows and denounced the practice of *sati*. He was impressed by the progressive thinking and rationalism of the Jat community in these matters.

Under the influence of the Arya Samaj, leaders of many other communities like the Vaisyas (Baniyas), the Brahmins and the Khatris made serious efforts to encourage widow remarriage in their communities, but met with little success. Strangely enough, the institutionalised custom of widow remarriage Jats have followed for long has received scant attention of sociologists and reformers. Consequently, it has not been highlighted in the manner it should have been in sociological narratives.

Rather, some authors, for instance, Krishan Chander, the eminent Punjabi novelist, has tried to cast the practice in poor light in his famous novel *Ek Chaadar Mailee See*, where he has tried to show that widow remarriage is unnatural and is imposed on the widow against her wishes.

However, having personally known many cases in the Jat community, I can say with authority that it is a fine and rational system, and has been working in the best interests of none other than the widows themselves. There can be no denying the fact that in exceptional cases, some excesses do take place, but that sort of difference between precept and practice is true of all customs, as well as laws universally.

It also needs to be recognised that a custom in vogue for a long time acquires greater force in terms of social acceptability than laws enacted by legislation for ensuring orderly and equitable human behaviour. The most outstanding aspect of customary laws is the in-built dispute resolution system (within the community), which is inexpensive, more transparent and certainly quicker as compared to the modern adversarial system of litigation.

The beauty of the community-based dispute resolution system is that the parties to the dispute approach the institution with a sense of submission; and once adjudicated, the dispute is resolved once and for all. There are no feelings of victory or defeat. In the modern adversarial system, one wins and the other loses, with inimical feeling lingering on.

All these dimensions call for a comprehensive study of such traditions so that some of their rational and beneficial elements can be incorporated into contemporary legal and judicial systems.

The Punjab High Court in its Lahore judgment (AIR 551, 1936, Jogender vs. Kartaaraa), having been influenced by the Brahmanical order and argument, classified Jats as Shudras in its judgment on the basis of *anulom* (when a woman of lower caste than that of the husband is taken in marriage) and *pratilom vivah* (the reverse of *anulom*, i.e., if a woman of a higher caste is taken in marriage).

Such marriages among Jats are not only permitted but also accepted completely without any reservation or stigma. Children from such unions are not refused in marriage. It again speaks volumes for the Jats' rationalism and progressivism.

Equally interesting and significant is the fact that Jats do take women of other castes, higher as well as lower, in marriage, but never give away their daughters to other castes traditionally.

It, therefore, needs to be emphasised that all these phenomena call for a fresh review. Sociologists and legal experts can then draw on elements of the community's customs that have served this important community well through the ages.

— (*Essay contributed by Sompal, former Union Minister and Member, Planning Commission*)

6

WANTED: A UN AGENCY FOR THE WELFARE OF WIDOWS

Widows and their children, the worst victims of human rights violations, need the attention of the United Nations without delay.

The United Nations Secretary-General Ban Ki-moon, to mark International Women's Day on March 8, 2010, asked the General Assembly to pass a resolution that would create a UN agency to focus solely on the well-being of women. In 2009, the UN announced that four agencies would be amalgamated to create one single agency that would be dedicated to the welfare of women. The agency would begin work with an annual budget of $1 billion.

"We hope soon to have a dynamic entity for gender equality and women's empowerment within the UN system.

That would provide more coherent programming and a stronger voice for women. ... I urge the General Assembly to create this new entity without delay by adopting a resolution," said Ban. He added that since the Beijing Declaration, marked progress had been made with a growing body of policy and legislation that sought to foster gender equality, reproductive health, employment and property rights.

But there was a word of caution. Ban Ki-moon noted that "gross violations of human rights against women persisted everywhere. In its worst form it manifests as violence. Up to 70 per cent of women experience violence in their lifetime. Most commonly, they are attacked by an intimate partner... We sometimes hear it said that such practices are a matter of culture. They are not. They are abuses and they are criminal and they deny women their fundamental rights."

Widows suffer no less. In fact, they have to endure the worst forms of violence—mental torture along with physical assaults. The Loomba Foundation, through its Widows Research Report and this book, has sought to highlight the fact that widows, who throughout the world are subjected to systemic violence, are also victims of deprivation and exploitation. They are also more liable to be inflicted by HIV/AIDS.

On International Women's Day, March 8, 2010, the UN AIDS agency (UNAIDS) launched a new programme called 'Agenda for Accelerated Country Action for Women, Girls, Gender Equality and HIV'. This requires governments to address gender inequalities that expose women and girls to the risks of HIV/AIDS, a fact also reiterated by Deputy Secretary-General Asha-Rose Migiro. However, societies were either unable or unwilling to talk about these inequalities as being the drivers of the epidemic. She also pointed out that cohesive action to help address these inequalities too had been lacking for a long time. The question is where do the 245 million widows worldwide and their children figure in this debate.

The situation could not have been more alarming. For instance, the incidence of HIV/AIDS among widows, either infected by their late husbands, or male relatives who force themselves on the hapless women, sometimes dictated by custom, is shocking. This book goes a step further. It presents findings that can, and often do, corroborate the complicity of state policy in letting the epidemic spread among women.

The two UN initiatives are commendable. But they are unlikely to help the cause of widows per se. For example, most measures taken by various UN agencies for the poverty-stricken and the aged have failed to redress the woes of widows. Besides, society is by and large ranged against them. Their own families treat them as outcasts and having been consigned to the margins of society they are seldom regarded as worthy of care and welfare.

Both the Loomba Report and this book establish decisively the fact that UN agencies tasked with the responsibility of eradicating poverty and discrimination—and which naturally include women—and even those totally focused on women, have failed widows and their children. They cannot be simply bracketed with women in general or the aged as has been historically and conventionally done. The Loomba Foundation report has shown how futile the measures for helping women and the aged have been in redeeming widows from their tragic circumstances.

What is worse is the fear that the UN might wake up to the hellish life of widows too late. The number of widows, especially the young, is growing alarmingly because of wars, regional and sectarian conflicts, terrorism and HIV/AIDS. The adverse effect on women because of the delay in setting up a dedicated UN agency for them has been criticised in many quarters.

As said earlier, widows have been bracketed with women in general, when in reality, widows seldom benefit from any welfare measures. The UN and governments around the world must bring to bear exclusive focus on the plight of widows. They are the worst victims of human rights violations.

Raj Loomba, Founder of the Loomba Foundation which has

been campaigning for the UN to officially adopt June 23 as International Widows Day, however, felt encouraged following the Secretary-General Ban Ki-moon's urgent call to the General Assembly to set up a UN agency for the welfare of women. Hopefully, Loomba said, the Secretary-General would likewise consider forming an exclusive agency for widows. Should it become a reality, it would easily get support of the governments of its 192 member-states.

"The Secretary-General, as he urged the setting up of a UN agency for the welfare of women on International Women's Day on March 8, 2010, could also officially declare June 23 as the International Widows Day and announce the formation of a UN agency for SALVATION of widows," Loomba observed.

Widows are women too. But they are never treated like women. Once the husband is dead, the widow is pushed to the margins of society, helpless, isolated, ridiculed, discriminated against and exploited. What is worse, a widow is regarded either as a bad omen, an outcast, a 'killer', a loose person or even a witch.

The 'UN Agency for Women' is a laudable initiative and is a step forward for gender equality and empowerment of women, but, widows need an exclusive UN agency not for gender equality alone but for restoration of their womanhood with dignity.

The rest will follow.

7

CONCLUSION

WIDOWHOOD: A HUMAN RIGHTS ISSUE

Empowerment is the only assured solution

Numerous instances and statistics of the agonising lives of widows in male-dominated closed and tradition-bound societies in developing countries and the economic decline, emotional trauma and social isolation in the developed West given in the earlier chapters clearly bring out why women, anywhere in the world, despise the word 'widow'. The loss of a husband deprives them of their basic human rights. The world owes it to them to take note of the deprivation, indignity and discrimination, which they suffer when widowed. Everyone, from international organisations to governments, from institutions to societies and people are obligated to ensure them their human rights as women.

This book and the 2009 Widows Research report provide the guidelines for what could and should be done to put together a support base for them and to restore their rightful place in society. Both have comprehensively investigated the torture widows are forced to endure and the consequences and manifestations of widowhood on their children. It has also been proved that measures governments have taken to bring succour to widows have been inadequate and ineffective. Thus the issue of widowhood, owing to long years of global nonchalance, has assumed critical urgency. The problems of widows are so complex and their number so huge that they can no longer be dealt with by individual governments alone.

The logical conclusion is that genuine redress of this humanitarian crisis is possible only if the United Nations takes the lead for a cohesive global effort. It calls for a global awareness of the problems widows face the world over, a change in peoples' perceptions, and a campaign for their empowerment so that they may live independently and with dignity. It also requires the reach, resources and influence of the UN and its agencies. The UN alone can persuade and co-opt governments in its endeavours and induce them to work for the salvation of widows. It is a just and humanitarian cause.

The UN and its agencies should comprehend and deal with the issues afflicting widows on a priority basis because widows continue to grow in number, more so those who are young. Conflicts, wars and the epidemic of HIV/AIDS in many parts of the globe have not only increased the number of widows, but also caused large-scale displacement among them. The torment of young widows, in particular, is compounded by exploitation. It has been shown that most victims of wars, terrorism and HIV/AIDS are young and once caught in bondage and inhuman circumstances, they seldom escape. Salvation comes only with death. Or suicide!

The UN has evidence, compiled by the Loomba

Foundation's worldwide survey, that most widows continue to be pushed to the margins of society and are subjected to innumerable indignities. The fact of the matter is that until now there has been no universal realisation (or acceptance) that their condition has shamed societies and for all those who profess to be protectors and champions of human rights of all without discrimination.

There is another alarming aspect. The Report estimated that in 2010 there were 245 million widows across the world. However, in remote areas in most developing countries many are left out of a census because they are either homeless or live in shelters.

One can imagine then the magnitude of the problem. If the number in reality is far more than 245 million, then their number along with that of their children—average of four each—could exceed a sixth of the world's population! Who can embark upon and take up the challenge of assisting such a large number? The answer is obvious—the United Nations which has the wherewithal to influence its 192 members.

The argument that efforts by a few UN agencies to help widows have been ineffective because of the lack of proper evidence about the abrupt changes in the status and circumstances of women when they become widows, can no longer hold. The Loomba Foundation has sought to eliminate the data hurdle by recording their conditions, both at the micro and macro levels across the globe. The fact is there has been an utter lack of concerted effort or determination to help them. It has also been exposed that governments, the international community, and civil society, and even many women's organisations, except for giving intermittent spells of support, have never really focused on the woes of widows and treated their predicament as a human rights issue.

The book has brought to the fore the fact that more widows have been aided by charities, NGOs and associations formed by Trusts and individuals in their respective areas than by laws that supposedly exist to ensure their rights. NGOs and private charities, however well intentioned, have been able to help only a fraction of the women. They are encumbered by limited resources and most are localised. But these organisations can be given special advisory and operational roles by the UN agencies once they focus, exclusively, on the empowerment and support of widows.

The book has attempted to bring these and other issues centrestage to make the world appreciate the magnitude of the problem, in the hope that the UN will take the initiative for a campaign on a global scale for governments and peoples to unite in tackling this human rights issue. Their rescue is not easy, for these women are subjected to a whole host of intractable problems linked to age-old customs, rituals, religious beliefs and avarice.

The Widows Research Report has also enumerated what can and must be done for salvaging widows from the margins of society. It concluded that "there is no all-embracing single solution—just as there isn't for poverty itself—but the first objective is to make this a global issue to be addressed by international governments."

It said: "Advocacy must be the way forward initially followed by action because the problem of widows' deprivation to date has been all but ignored." As stated earlier, few attempts at the international level to address the issue have succeeded in rescuing them from bizarre customs and rites that in fact violate the human rights of the widows and their dependants.

It has also been shown that despite several constraints, NGOs like the Loomba Foundation, Oxfam, The Prince's Trust, Help Age International, Widows Rights International, charities and welfare associations in many countries have been doing their best; however, their reach being naturally circumscribed, the UN must take up the issue on a truly global scale.

The Widows Research Report has collated most information about widows and their problems. Many academics have also carried out excellent research and have published books that provide insights into the travails of widows in various societies. All of these can provide sufficient background material and information for the UN to plan and implement measures for the welfare of widows.

Women's associations, NGOs and charities too have data, but naturally all these relate to specific regions within the country they operate. Yet, once compiled together the statistics and findings would be of immense value to the UN and its agencies.

"The reports by analysts, academics and the 2009 Loomba Foundation Report on Widows can all be excellent guidelines for more in-depth inquiry into the state of widows, particularly in Africa and India," says Raj Loomba. In some countries, such as China, Cambodia and Vietnam, information about widows is sketchy. The UN could persuade them to give up their reluctance to part with the relevant data so that support could reach them as well. All these steps are required to comprehend, in its totality, the consequences of widowhood the world over.

The rites, customs and practices that deprive widows of their legitimate rights are hardly known universally. Thus, there is no global awareness of their plight, which is necessary if a joint effort is to be made for the cause of widows.

The objectives outlined by the National Association of Widows in Britain underline the problems widows face in the West. Widowhood has been described as the "single-most common personal catastrophe. This catastrophe is a bereavement which affects women physically and socially as well as emotionally."

The National Association of Widows was founded in 1971 by June Hermer, who was herself a widow, in order to give all widows the specialist information, advice and support they needed. "If you are a widow you may find that you need: the chance to contact other widows; someone to listen to without being judgemental; company and the chance for a better social life; help with practical matters and unconditional support." The fact that widows in the West do also need support is a telling commentary on the state of widows in any part of the world, developed or developing.

On the other hand, there is little awareness in the developed world about the tragedy of widows in developing countries. Except in Britain, in particular, where the Loomba Foundation has helped generate awareness about the condition of widows in India and Africa.

The work being done by the Foundation, for example, in a few African countries, has shown tangible results. This was only possible because the Governments there became aware of the Foundation's interest in helping the cause of widows and offered full cooperation.

The importance of generating awareness in the developed world about the tragic lives of widows in the developing world cannot be overstated. Only then will Governments, corporations, Foundations, Financial Institutions, Trusts and charities be persuaded to contribute to welfare measures being undertaken in the developing countries. This is where the role of the UN and its agencies becomes critical.

Another major handicap in helping or even understanding the problems of widows is that no effort has so far been made to categorise widows according to the cause of the demise of their husbands—natural death, wars, HIV/AIDS or accidents—and then explore all possible avenues to get relief to them.

The Loomba Foundation has launched awareness campaigns in several countries and has also set an example by showing how quickly widows can be empowered to be independent and command respect. It has also been observing June 23 as the International Widows Day every year in more than six countries. It is also educating 3,000 children of poor widows in India. This has given them a purpose in life, and to their widowed mother's hope.

As said earlier, however, considering the complex

problems, social, political and financial, the number of widows worldwide, and the reluctance of people to give up age-old customs and religious beliefs, any effective resolution of the misery of widows and their dependants can only be on a global scale.

This is possible, to reiterate, only if the UN and its agencies take up the cause of widows exclusively and not bracket them with the poverty-stricken or the aged. Plans have also got to be country-specific. Admittedly, the issue is complex and, therefore, requires solutions that can effectively address problems specific to developing countries on the one hand and developed countries on the other. Each region requires customised solutions.

But if the UN declares the problem of widows as a human rights issue, its member-states can come together to tackle not only problems that are basic and common, like loss of status and income or isolation, but also those that are country-specific. Some initiatives, such as those by the Food and Agriculture Organisation against poverty, and HIV/AIDS campaigns by others, have embraced issues that were also relevant to widows. But these were all encompassing in nature and therefore not the most effective way of tackling problems faced by widows. The reality is that nothing tangible has been done at the international level to tackle forced disinheritance, property and land "grabbing", ritual cleansing, enforced sex with relatives and social stigmatising.

Even when widows have been, by law, given rights, they are often simply unaware of them (being often illiterate) or are unable to demand justice because of poverty. Yet, Governments have done little either to ensure that widows are educated about their rights, or are provided with support structures to help them secure those rights.

In sub-Saharan Africa, HIV/AIDS, ethnic cleansing and violent strife between tribes have widowed many young and middle-aged women. The Widows Research Report cites the case study of an Eritrean widow, 47-year-old Kidan Felmon, whose husband was a well-to-do merchant. She was confident that she would not face any financial crisis and that she would be able to look after her nine children comfortably. But her hope was short-lived. She found out that her husband had AIDS and that she was herself infected by him.

The right of inheritance and the liberty to use it are also denied, as is the right to remarry someone of their choice. "Disinheritance in the context of widow inheritance (levirate) has become a prominent issue for widows as a result of the HIV/AIDS crisis" (Widows Research Report, 2009, p. 26). Women face disinheritance because of the fact that in a number of Asian and sub-Saharan countries laws have not been standardised and inheritance is decided on the basis of customary and religious laws. This is true in Ghana, Zambia and Zimbabwe. In Namibia, widow inheritance (forced marriage to a relative) by a husband's brother is illegal, and so is forced disinheritance, but in practice the widow does not benefit because of the weak legal system.

This reinforces the argument that countrywide outreach services are crucial in countries where there is low Government penetration in vast swathes of rural and urban areas. Typically, in such areas, there is inadequate information and understanding of marriage and inheritance laws, adversely impacting widows and their children.

It has also been found that wherever statutory law exists, awareness does not, customary law is imposed in countries where it is still practised, particularly in most of the developing countries. These customary laws, as instances showed, place widows at a significant disadvantage, in either laying claim to their legitimate rights or resisting oppression and suppression.

Also, rural areas are typically where poverty manifests itself in most societies. Therefore, no development strategy of any kind can be successful without designing interventions capable of penetrating these areas. In India, for instance, many remote villages and settlements are difficult to reach. Similar is the situation in Africa. In both the number of widows is huge.

Another key issue that has to be kept in focus is that socially and geographically isolated and illiterate populations are more often unaware of the existence of available government services and of the role of law. This has hampered widows in most countries like Uganda or Kenya from recourse to anti-discrimination laws.

Only a professional social worker can understand how illiteracy and poverty affect widows. For example, income support for widows is available for those under age 60, together with other conditions.

A similar set of dynamics in Bangladesh led to the development of an NGO called BRAC. BRAC has grown to provide comprehensive services, and on a large scale, to the extent that it has tacit acceptance by the Government as playing the part of the Government's role as service provider.

In India the proposal to reserve 33 per cent of seats for women in Parliament and state Assemblies would also be a stimulus for enforcement of laws protecting widows' rights. As was mentioned earlier, the local bodies, with greater representation of women have helped widows to inherit the property and assets of her late husband. In fact, within the 33 per cent reservation, a quota for widows would go a long way in empowering them.

Women's Bureaux in several Southern and East African countries have been pressing—and some have carried them out—for changes in inheritance laws to protect widows. Changes in Penal Codes have also been carried out, making it an offence to discriminate against a widow or deprive her of her rights.

There is thus huge country-specific information available. If all of the countries were to come together under the aegis of the UN and its agencies, all relevant statistics on a global scale would be at its disposal. Its agencies can then instantly understand problems faced by widows the world over, the reasons for those problems, the measures and laws available for redress, and a complete list of organisations engaged in assisting widows in each and every country. These are, however, time-consuming and require sustained efforts. No cut and paste solution is possible, because the world has glossed over their state and neglected them for too long.

However, governments have to take the first step by providing the capacity at the level of ministries for the reforms to take place. The initiative for encouraging governments to do so would also have to come from the UN. It has a wonderful example in Namibia. It has taken a robust approach to legal reform both in letter and spirit. The country's constitution "... has been widely praised for its strong commitment to human rights and its specific focus on gender equality and the rights of women. The constitution also uses gender-neutral language throughout and forbids discrimination on the basis of sex."[1]

As with many former colonies, Namibia has laws that predate its 1990 constitution, and which are at odds with the constitution. Therefore, Namibia took the next step, in 1992 and "...established a statutory body, the Law Reform and Development Commission, whose mandate is to review all discriminatory legislation and to make proposals for its amendment."

Crucially, "a Women and Law Committee was established under this commission to give special attention to law reform on gender-related matters."[2]

The other key factor in promoting reform, both from the point of view of either having to lobby governments to begin the process, or to assist an ongoing process by providing case study information, is the NGO sector.

With respect to developing countries, Uganda is cited as an example of a country with a strong women's movement (comprising NGOs and broad-based women's activism). The 1998 Land Act saw agreement reached by the Ugandan parliament to allow the right to land co-ownership by husbands and wives, though the published version of the Act omitted any such mention. The Ugandan women's movement has since maintained pressure on the issue, and as of 2002, although not having been resolved in favour of equality, "the issue of women and land has become a 'hot topic,' thanks in large part to the advocacy by women and non-governmental organisations..."[3]

One major step forward would be for governments to provide financial assistance to widows approaching the courts of law. At present, this is being done on a small scale by NGOs like CWCA in Tanzania or the Women's Centre for Legal Aid and Counselling in Jerusalem for Palestinian women.[4]

Another measure that would help governments to help widows take recourse to rights available to them is to make registration of all marriages compulsory and legally binding. This is crucial if widows are to be protected from avaricious family members who grab her inheritance. In most countries in sub-Saharan Africa, unregistered marriages are common, while registration is required for inheritance.[5]

Registration is also essential if the widows are to be helped to claim and enforce property rights. Even in India there has been no such law. It is only now that moves are on to make registration compulsory. Here again, the rural hinterland, in particular, would require the services of professional social workers. Otherwise illiterate or poor women would have no knowledge about the law, whenever enacted. Reform of property and inheritance rights also requires reforms in marriage laws in order to give women greater bargaining power vis-à-vis husbands and family members.

Once a marriage is registered it would be easier to claim land and property rights. Most countries now have laws guaranteeing inheritance rights to a widow. There is, however, still the problem of determining the system under which women can remarry (customary versus civil law). That determines whether women can inherit property so long as the civil law also grants women's rights to property ownership and inheritance. This will change the incentives guiding intra-household gender relations by changing the material outcome of widowhood itself. International development agencies (bilateral, multilateral and NGOs) would have to put aside their specific strategic interests and pool practical resources, as well as conduct coordinated planning and assign designated roles for programme delivery.

This proposal goes some way in making real the vague language of the last Millennium Development Goal No. 7, which focuses on the need to propose practical action, but does not map out possible starting points for such action.

Food security is a priority too. Indeed, it is a critical issue for widows and their children in developing countries, in particular in the least developed countries (LDCs), because most of them are involved in subsistence agriculture for their livelihood. In fact, a high proportion of people in India, Bangladesh and in many developing countries are dependent on subsistence agriculture. They are at high risk of food shortages, and in some cases famines, owing to climatic conditions, natural disasters, soil fertility exhaustion, international trade rules on agriculture, and trade rules on structural adjustment.

The other problem is that widows mostly get small holdings, after partition of the property left by her husband, for the husband himself could have got a small share when the family assets were divided. Such holdings provide for bare subsistence. In such cases widows and their children run the risk of starvation if there are droughts, floods or other disasters. Floods are regular occurrences in Bangladesh.

A significant problem in sub-Saharan African countries affected by HIV/AIDS is the unavailability of ready farm labour, a situation brought about by high male and female adult mortality. In Cambodia and Vietnam, widows are totally dependent on agriculture.

These are the core issues, all of which have been voiced by researchers, NGOs and some governments. Of these, the one issue with the potential to have immediate and far-reaching impact on most widows is international trade with regard to agriculture. This too needs the focus of the United Nations.

Developed country subsidies on agricultural production and export (which also hurt their own residents through higher and wasted taxes), together with import restrictions, have significantly damaged food security in developing countries. At the same time, through the structural adjustment programmes of the World Bank, developing countries have been forced to liberalise their trade rules to accommodate imports from developed countries. Developed countries have not reciprocated.

Kevin Watkins, until recently Director of the United Nations Human Development Report, and a former head of research at Oxfam GB, writes: "Developing countries have been liberalising rapidly, while rich countries, despite the free trade rhetoric of their governments, have remained fiercely protectionist in their approach to developing country exports. These protectionist polices are one reason why integration into world markets is not delivering its full benefits to poor countries."[6]

The impact on widows, "poor people in general and women in particular bear the brunt, since it is they who produce the goods most affected by import barriers: agriculture and labour-intensive manufactured goods. Agriculture accounts for 62 per cent of women's employment in developing countries, and women make up 70 per cent of workers in export-processing zones."[7] There is, therefore, an extremely strong case for immediate action on developed country trade polices in agriculture.

In sum, one can say with conviction that the only way to counter obscurantist traditions, social customs, general nonchalance, isolation, discrimination, oppression and exploitation—sometimes barbaric—affecting widows is by empowering them. Only then can they fully appreciate their entitlements and be able to pursue their claims through legal processes available to them.

Widows have been quick learners and are eager and cooperative whenever offered vocational training. The Loomba Foundation has, in particular, been focusing on this aspect. Its schemes for the empowerment of widows has been widely recognised for offering a significant advance in breaking the vicious cycle of poverty widows find themselves in.

The positive effects of empowering widows economically have already been demonstrated. It has been shown that higher income earning capacity among women improves human capital: Significantly more income in the hands of mothers goes directly to children's health and education than income in the hands of fathers.[8]

Also, under the current set of social norms in many developing countries, the consequences of widowhood represent a depreciation of the productive assets of these economies, and therefore represent a deduction from the total value of their GDPs. The perverse perception that widows are liabilities needs to change.

The key outcomes that should help empower widows are:

- Generate international awareness among researchers, policy specialists, politicians, NGOs and the public of the significance of widows' deprivation
- Institute inheritance and property ownership rights
- Generate awareness of law on marriage and inheritance and of welfare measures provided by governments and NGOs
- Provide government support in the form of income and healthcare, free education and childcare costs immediately after women are widowed
- Recognise the instrumental value of empowerment and implement literacy programmes for widows
- Help check HIV/AIDS infection on a priority basis
- Help transform male attitudes

The initiatives required for achieving the above for the empowerment of widows and securing their well-being and that of their children are, among others:

- Recognition of June 23 as the International Widows Day from the point of view of advocacy
- Reform of country-level legal systems to ensure inheritance rights for widows and also ensure that widows can seek legal recourse to claim the assured rights
- Provision of countrywide outreach services
- Reform and expansion of welfare states to provide effective social security for widows
- Emergency aid for the HIV/AIDS belt of eastern and southern sub-Saharan Africa, to include food, health, and agriculture support services and inputs, and systematic HIV/AIDS prevention plans
- Recognition of widows as the last line of defence in HIV/AIDS ravaged communities and supporting them accordingly
- Literacy programmes to be women-run at the point of delivery, utilisation of NGO networks[9] and the micro-finance model as an organisational model for delivery of actual tuition[10]
- Achieve country-level food security that has a direct impact on the lives of widows and their children. This would include the immediate abolition of current agricultural trade rules and practices by OECD and EU countries with respect to developing countries, especially dumping, export subsidies, and developing country market access to OECD and EU, with necessary reforms to WTO
- Gender mainstreaming in policy systems where women's social and economic issues will also cover widows and their children

International Widows Day: The Starting Point

The recognition of International Widows Day by the UN would highlight the plight of impoverished widows throughout the world and herald the official date and day on the agenda of mainstream humanitarian causes.

Such recognition would only be a beginning. But it would be a start on the long road to empowering widows and in effect help begin a journey towards restoring human rights to nearly a sixth of the world's population.

Why is it imperative that there has to be a United Nations International Widows Day? The Loomba Foundation thus submits:

- It is a fundamental step in disseminating awareness about the seriousness and scale of the deprivation faced by widows and their children across the world
- A critical tool in drawing attention to the links between the causes of widows' deprivation and the crucial areas of women and children's health, education, and empowerment
- An effective instrument to mobilise opinion that the welfare of widows would be a crucial determinant of the success of the Millennium Development Goals

By itself, the International Widows Day will not mark the end of the plight of widows and their children, for it would only be the beginning of hope for them. The UN, governments and people would have to be determined to sustain their joint campaign and efforts to redeem their sins of omission.

(Extracts from the Widows Research Report used and incorporated)

ENDNOTES

[1] One World Action (2001: 40).

[2] One World Action (2001: 41).

[3] Asiimwe (2002: 121).

[4] Women's Centre for Legal Aid and Counselling (1995).

[5] For specifics in relation to the effects on property of marriage under customary versus formal marriage registration, see Horrell et al (2007: 1353-1355) on female-headed household in Zimbabwe.

[6] Oxfam International (2002: 95).

[7] Oxfam International (2002: 96), citing Chen et al (1999).

[8] Chant (2007: 335); Todaro and Smith (2009: 22).

[9] Example of an NGO network focused on women's development is the grassroots women's organisation called Sangtin, Sitapur district, central Uttar Pradesh state, India, see Sangtin Writers and Nagar (2006: xxii).

[10] Relevance of the micro-finance model to academic activity is through the former's use of positive peer pressure to maintain the operation of the group; in the micro-finance case, the personal, small-group dynamics ensure women repay loans, while in the literacy teaching case, it is used to ensure that literacy group members maintain attendance and complete the required work.

ANNEXURE I

Widows' Deprivation and Poverty

Using internationally recognised sources of data and measurement techniques, the Loomba Foundation has been able to put together the following picture of widows' deprivation and poverty.

Out of at least 245 million widows around the world:

1. Over 100 million widows live in extreme poverty where basic needs go unmet, causing a downward spiral of malnutrition, deteriorating health and starvation and physical insecurity, such as risk of HIV/AIDS and rape.
2. The most dire conditions are faced by Afghan and Iraqi widows (numbering around 2 million and at least 740,000 respectively) because of ongoing conflict; in sub-Saharan African countries by evicted widows with children; by elderly widows caring for orphaned grandchildren in HIV/AIDS crisis countries; and by child widows—from ages 7 to 17—in developing countries.
3. Another 57.4 million widows exist in moderate poverty, just above those in extreme poverty, where the basic needs are mostly-to-only-just met. In total there are 116.7 million widows in all types of poverty globally, or 47 per cent of all widows.
4. Dependent children—at least 17 per cent of widows have dependent children up to age 17, rising to a high of 36 per cent in South Asia. Europe (east and west, including Russia) and North America have the lowest, with 7.6 per cent and 5.2 per cent respectively.
5. Cleansing rituals—rituals are performed to "cleanse" widows after the death of their husbands, amounting to trial-by-ordeal. These are based around beliefs to do with the afterlife and suspicion about widows surviving their husbands. They can involve the widow having to drink the water used to wash the dead husband's body, and sexual intercourse with a relative. The latter is high risk in countries with high levels of HIV/AIDS. Ritual cleansing has been reported in sub-Saharan Africa, in Angola, Botswana, Republic and Democratic Republic of Congo,

Cote d'lvoire, Ghana, Kenya, Lesotho, Malawi, Nigeria, Rwanda, Senegal, Swaziland, Tanzania, Uganda, Zambia, and Zimbabwe.

6. Suspicion of murder—widows in South Asia and sub-Saharan Africa are often erroneously accused of murdering their husbands or causing their deaths through insufficient care—particularly where death has been caused by HIV/AIDS.
7. Widow evictions and property theft—forced eviction from the family home and seizure of even the most meagre of cooking utensils by the late husband's family are widespread.
8. Elderly widows left to run society—elderly widows are increasingly the last adults left to bring up children following the devastation of communities by HIV/AIDS, which has reached crisis levels in eastern and southern Africa. Countries facing particular emergencies include Botswana, with an adult 15-49 age group infection rate of 23.9 per cent, South Africa with 21.5 per cent, Zimbabwe with 24.6 per cent, Swaziland with 38.8 per cent, and Zambia with 16.5 per cent. In India, total HIV/AIDS infections among all age 15 and above are 2.6 million,[1] compared to South Africa's 5.7 million.
9. Western Widows—in developed countries such as the USA, widows with low educational qualifications face lives of severe insecurity due to lack of affordable health care and the erosion of well paid jobs for low skilled workers. President Obama observed that many Americans were "one medical emergency away from bankruptcy," a characteristic of developing countries. In Eastern Europe, Central Asia and Russia, welfare states have been eroded significantly since 1990, leading to similar insecurity for widows with low qualifications and low incomes.

In addition to these broad trends, widows and their children suffer from a range of less well documented but extremely serious outcomes as a result of the loss of husbands and partners. These issues embrace poverty, health, human rights and child protection, with consequences ranging from exposure to serious diseases and over-work, to targeted murder, forced marriage, child marriage, children's loss of schooling, child labour, and multiple child safety risks (trafficking and street living), including child rape.

These consequences stem from the immediate loss of income that tips widows and their children into poverty, as well as its impact in the deepening of poverty for families already experiencing a degree of poverty. Hazardous work, loss of paid work for widows due to care giving responsibilities and employer discrimination, lack of government social service provision across the full spectrum of needs, harmful traditional practices, illiteracy, preventable disease and inadequate post-conflict security all add to the widows' pot of misery.

ENDNOTE

[1] Wilson and Claeson (2009: 14-17).

ANNEXURE II

Number of Widows and How Widowhood is Defined

Table numbers below correspond to the original numbering in the Loomba Foundation Widows Research Report 2009. The regional widows data projections for 2010 for total widows and widows in extreme and moderate poverty are presented.

Widows are measured in the number of un-remarried widows, as opposed to the number of un-remarried and remarried widows (data for the latter are typically not collected for most countries). The age range for widows and hence marriage, varies greatly between regions.

Table 2.1. Regional Data for Widows and Extreme Poverty, 2010

Region, Percent of age group	Total Widows	Extreme Pov	Moderate Pov	Total Poverty
North Africa	5,821,360	166,232	877,646	1,043,878
Middle East	12,579,368	836,735	1,425,585	2,262,320
Sub-Saharan Africa (all countries)	20,985,961	10,783,653	4,764,939	15,548,592
Sub-Saharan Africa AIDS crisis countries	5,370,434	2,783,727	895,188	3,678,915
Sub-Saharan Africa non-AIDS crisis	16,348,543	8,434,696	4,012,959	12,447,655
Central Asia	3,626,846	1,429,534	1,491,464	2,920,998
South Asia	54,482,268	21,977,809	18,380,907	40,358,716
East Asia and Pacific	79,140,501	11,917,410	16,183,125	28,100,535
South East Asia	23,551,502	4,617,876	5,972,725	10,590,601
North East Asia	54,530,538	7,280,665	10,104,192	17,384,857
Advanced East Asia	11,275,231	111,635	1,077,830	1,189,465
Pacific Islands	38,551	11,565	9,561	21,126
Anglo Pacific Islands	1,019,910	1,318	8,569	9,887
Caribbean	854,943	147,043	87,847	234,890
North America	14,841,788	564,129	712,548	1,276,677

(Contd.)

Table 2.1. (*Contd.*)

Region, Percent of age group	Total Widows	Extreme Pov	Moderate Pov	Total Poverty
Central America	3,700,909	165,676	171,485	337,161
South America	11,256,143	1,457,304	1,593,350	3,050,654
Europe (all) incl. Russia	43,719,903	1,397,599	7,704,966	9,102,565
West Europe	23,107,938	188,519	2,156,735	2,345,254
Scandinavia (Europe)	1,235,268	8,107	59,890	67,997
Eastern Europe incl. Russia	18,479,621	1,209,080	5,548,230	6,757,310
OECD High Income countries	48,492,091	848,832	3,905,114	4,753,946
Least Developed Countries	25,594,090	17,690,805	3,121,063	20,811,868
Totals	245,188,630	59,277,820	57,406,821	116,684,641

Table Note: See Appendix for individual countries under each regional grouping. Data source, Loomba Foundation (2009) estimates using World Bank (2008b) and individual countries' poverty data and UN Population Division for 2010 and individual countries' demographic data.

Conventions in the way data on marital status are collected means that for developed countries, widows' (and marital status) data start from age 15, while in developing countries, it starts from as low as 10 years of age.

The global total of widows (un-remarried), is over 245 million for the year 2010. East Asia and Pacific, which includes Australia and New Zealand, accounts for the most widows by region, at over 79 million; the second and third most significant regions are South Asia and Europe, including Russia, at around 55 million and 43 million respectively. The smallest number of widows is found in the Caribbean, with circa 855,000.

In percentage terms, the largest group of widows can be found in Europe, including Russia, and Central Asia, while the Caribbean has the smallest percentage share of widows by region. The global corresponding group of women to which widows are compared is just over 2.7 billion.

Table 2.2. Regional Widows Percentage Shares, 2010

Region	Women's Population,* 2010, by Corresponding age range of widows	Widows percentage of Corresponding Women's Population, 2010
North America	142,358,400	10.4
Central America	55,677,600	6.6
Caribbean	13,562,173	6.3
South America	159,543,000	7.1
Europe incl. Russia	328,084,000	13.3
Mid East and North Africa	170,307,800	7.4

(*Contd.*)

Table 2.2. (*Contd.*)

Region	Women's Population,* 2010, by Corresponding age range of widows	Widows percentage of Corresponding Women's Population, 2010
Sub-Saharan Africa	298,308,269	7.0
Central Asia	30,120,600	12.0
South Asia	618,729,000	8.8
East Asia and Pacific	920,705,379	8.6
Total	2,737,396,221	9.0

*See Loomba Foundation Widows Research Report (2009) for individual country data tables on widows totals per country for precise age ranges for individual countries used. These age ranges are set by national statistics departments.

Data source, Loomba Foundation (2009) estimates using UN Population Division for 2010 and individual countries' demographic data.

Table 2.5. Top 20 Countries with the Highest Number of Widows, 2010

Country	Region	Total Number Widows	Widows % of Corresponding Female Population
China	North East Asia	43,044,943	8.1
India	South Asia	42,395,063	9.1
USA	North America	13,593,000	10.5
Indonesia	South East Asia	9,448,286	8.1
Japan	North East Asia	7,398.791	13.0
Russia	Europe/Asia	7,071,647	11.0
Brazil	South America	5,569,586	6.7
Germany	Western Europe	5,111,621	14.0
Bangladesh	South Asia	4,728,275	7.3
Vietnam	South East Asia	4,685,716	10.4
Pakistan	South Asia	4,333,759	7.6
Ukraine	Eastern Europe	4,107,635	19.0
Italy	Western Europe	4,034,769	15.0
France	Western Europe	3,456,183	13.0
Egypt	North Africa	3,446,855	12.0
Nigeria	Sub-Saharan Africa	3,443,029	6.2
UK	Western Europe	3,284,886	13.0
Thailand	South East Asia	3,065,182	8.8
Philippines	South East Asia	2,901,402	6.2
Mexico	Central America	2,898,346	6.6

Table Note: Data source, Loomba Foundation (2009) estimates using UN Population Division for 2010 and individual countries' demographic data.

ANNEXURE III

Poverty Cause of Widowhood

Figure 2.3 shows the relationship between extreme (absolute) poverty and the incidence of widows per country. The steadily increasing line is a ranking, in order of severity per country, of extreme poverty. The line that moves erratically up and down between zero and 20 per cent is the percentage of widows per country corresponding to the rank of the country in extreme poverty. The numbered horizontal axis simply shows the cumulative number of countries, the world total of 193.[1]

Figure 2.3. Widows and Poverty

Global Picture: Extreme Poverty and Widows Incidence, 2010, all countries (percent, rank)

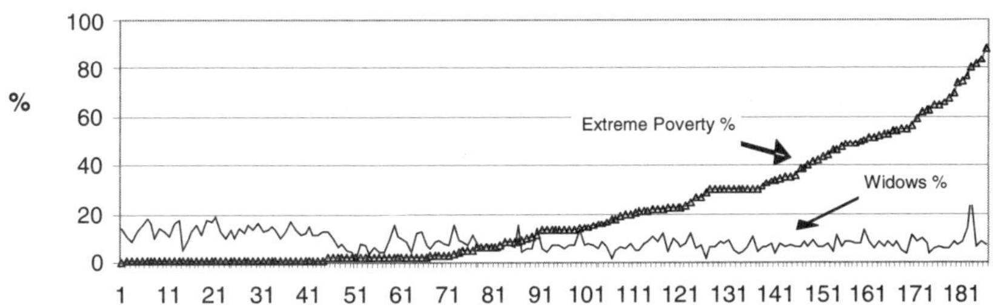

Extreme Poverty and Widows: country extreme poverty rank (extreme poverty worsens to the right, reaching above 80% of a country's population, measured on vertical scale, left), with corresponding per country widows percentage of women's population (up and down jagged line, percentage also measured at right.)

Chart Note: Data Sources, widows (Loomba Foundation), poverty World Bank (2008b): demographic data for 2010, UN Population Division.

Poverty as a cause of widowhood is of interest because it acts to cause premature widowhood. Premature widowhood is a serious concern, because it has intergenerational consequences, characterised by women with dependent children. It is also a serious concern given the high reported incidence in widows under age 60 in many developing countries. These women themselves are particularly or wholly dependent on husbands and partners as the primary source of economic support. Crucially, premature widowhood is more frequent in countries where government support in the form of income support and free healthcare is poor or not available at all, and in several regions, women's paid employment is either low paid, or socially unacceptable.[2] Becoming a widow under these conditions can therefore lead to a fall into poverty, or a deepening of existing poverty. Poverty therefore sets the scene and enables the conditions for people with low human and social capital and low economic and financial assets to fall into a range of deprivations. Poverty is a breeding ground for disease, and in so doing, reinforces itself. Poverty also sets the constraints that prevent such people from pulling themselves above the poverty quicksand.

In turn, poverty or a fall in living standards, can lead to self-destructive psycho-social results, especially for men, leading to increased premature male mortality and hence early widowhood.[3] Clearly, widows' circumstances in most developing countries put them at high risk of poverty, and additional acute direct threats to their well-being. Vulnerability in East Europe also appears to be significant, as well as in Central Asia and parts of Latin America and East Asia; while the picture is more favourable in most advanced OECD countries.

ENDNOTES

[1] Note that this is the case if Palestine is assumed a de facto country. The data above, and elsewhere in this report include Palestine. Officially, however, there are 192 recognised stales. Other de facto states seeking recognition are Somaliland, Puntland, and Western Sahara, see *The World Guide*, New Internationalist Publications (2007).

[2] Includes Afghanistan before, during and after the Taleban, as one aid worker observed while serving in Afghanistan during the Soviet war in the 1980s, "the division of between male and female society was rigid....male visitors [to Afghan homes] could not enter the [main] house, [were not permitted to physically see] see any women or even talk about them," Vaux (2001: 116); during the Taleban see Marsden (1998). Extensively cited in research, in northern India, Pakistan and Bangladesh, employment outside the home for pay, and regular movement outside the home village is a serious problem for women, who risk serious damage to reputation, and physical violence as punishment from relatives. In contrast, in China, millions of teenage rural girls migrate to work in factories, see Chang (2008).

[3] This has been seen across Eastern Europe, and especially in Russia, since 1990.

ANNEXURE IV

Hazardous Work, Disease and Chronic Poor Health

"Work Kills More People Than Wars"

The International Labour Organization (ILO) estimates that each year there are 2.3 million deaths of workers, or approximately 6 thousand a day, in part the result of the annual 270 million workplace accidents. Work deaths are defined as deaths arising from accidents and from illness caused by work. The ILO states, "work kills more people than wars", globally it costs 4 per cent of GDP, while the accident rate has been increasing in developing countries where an unknown number of work deaths goes unreported because a large proportion takes place in the informal sector of the economy.[1]

Poverty frequently contributes to high premature male mortality, hence widowhood, through hazardous work. Hazardous work is often exploitative, because low skill workers have *no* bargaining power[2] in many countries. As a result, hazardous work-related deaths become more likely when men have low skills and low or no education, or limited local opportunities to use more advanced skills.[3]

"Studies of occupational safety and health suggest an enormous toll in mortality and morbidity throughout the developing world, with very high costs.

A regular source of reported work deaths is in mining where, in particular, Chinese and Russian mining deaths are frequently in international news headlines.[4] A western journalist investigating Chinese mining accidents reports:

> "[Mining] accidents are so common in China that their plight and that of tens of thousands of other mining widows has become one of the most sensitive issues facing the communist government. More than 5,000 Chinese miners are killed each year, 75% of the global total, even though the country produces only a third of the world's coal. Working under appalling safety conditions, they are sacrificed to fuel the factories that make the cheap goods snapped up by consumers in Britain and other wealthy nations."[5]

The ILO explicitly backs the conclusion that worker deaths are disproportionately a poor *man's* burden: "Industrialised countries must take part of the blame. 'In fact', ILO specialist Jukka Takala says, 'one of the trends is that industrialised countries are exporting their hazards to developing countries. Labour there is not only cheaper but also significantly less protected. Dirty and difficult jobs are left to the South [developing countries]. That includes mining, of course.'" So while the mining diseases commonly known as pneumoconiosis, including silicosis, [dust caused illness] have virtually disappeared in the industrialised countries, they are still claiming fresh victims every day in the developing world."[6] The ILO reports that 6 million miners in Brazil, nearly 2 million in Colombia and more than 2 million in India are exposed to conditions that cause silicosis. In Latin America, 37 per cent of all miners are ill with silicosis.

The Impact of HIV/AIDS

Disease as a cause of widowhood does not operate on its own in a social vacuum.[7] In fact, social norms, and by this is meant socially learnt behaviours, are crucial as a facilitator of disease as a killer of men and hence cause of widowhood. Data on cause of male death bears this out. Table 2.7 presents data on the top five global causes of death for men aged 15-59 in Low- and Middle-income versus High-income countries.[8] Each top five group accounts for 56.5 per cent and 69.7 per cent of deaths respectively for these two country groupings. Causes of death heavily influenced by behaviour are represented for both Low- and Middle-income and High-income countries, notably road accidents, self-inflicted injuries and HIV/AIDS.

The impact of unprotected sex and the link with HIV/AIDS through prostitutes, in addition to other forms of frequent changing of sexual contacts, is now a major contributory factor to premature death.

The effects of this, and similarly rampant sexual promiscuity of men with women outside the sex trade on widows and their children are particularly fiercely felt in sub-Saharan Africa. East Asia has also been identified as a prostitution-HIV/AIDS hotspot. Thailand has been a noted case for many years given its huge sex industry, with reports of increasing HIV/AIDS infected husbands from middle class backgrounds. Meanwhile a reported upsurge in prostitution linked to changes in men's behaviour towards sexual activity has been reported in Vietnam. This change in Vietnamese male behaviour has been linked to the expansion of sex tourism in Vietnam since its economic reforms started in 1986. The Philippines is also a noted prostitution hotspot, hence a breeding ground for HIV/AIDS.[9]

Table 2.7 Male Premature Death Top Five Causes, percent of Annual Deaths 2001, ages 15-59

Death Cause	Low-, Mid.-income	Death Cause	High-income
1: Cardiovascular Disease	18.5	1: Cancer	27.7
2: HIV/AIDS	13.0	2: Cardiovascular Disease	23.4
3: Cancer	10.7	3: Self-inflicted injuries	8.5
4: Tuberculosis	7.8	4: Road Traffic Accidents	7.9
5: Road Traffic Accidents	6.5	5: Respirator,' Disease	2 2

Table Note: data source is Lopez et al (2006). The World Bank.

At the regional level, HIV/AIDS is the fourth leading cause of death in low and middle-income countries, while the disease is the leading cause of death for everyone in the 15-59 age group in sub-Saharan Africa.[10]

ENDNOTES

[1] ILO (2004); Hamalainen et al (2009).

[2] Trade unionists are routinely murdered in a number of countries because employers do not want to treat workers fairly.

[3] Quote by Stillwaggon (1998: 262), who cites Mohan (1993: 12-13) on Indian agriculture. "In Mexico, field workers on tomato farms that export produce to the United States market suffer from nervous disorders from organophosphatc poisoning. To prevent workers from going to local doctors, who are required to report the poisonings, foremen treat workers in the field with a temporary antidote, atropine."

[4] At the time of writing, July 2009, a Chinese mining accident was reported.

[5] Watts (2005). http://www.guardian.co.uk/world/2005/mar/14/china.jonathanwatts

[6] ILO (2004), preceding quote and following silicosis data.

[7] Todaro and Smith (2009: 400) note: "Poverty plays such a central role in most health problems faced by developing countries that it has its own designation in the International Classification of Diseases: code Z59.5 - extreme poverty."

[8] Data from Tables 3B. 1 and 3B.8. Lopez el al (2006: 126-130: 168-172).

[9] See Barry (1996: 144-156). In all three cases. The expansion in the sex industry is linked to foreign exchange access promoted by their respective tourist industries. This is well documented in the case of Thailand.

[10] Lopez et al (2006) pages 69 and 71 on fourth leading cause, and leading cause respectively.

Countries with Large Numbers of War Widows

Table 2.9. War Widows Countries—Part I

Sub-Saharan Africa	North Africa	Middle East	Central Asia	South Asia	East Asia
Angola	Algeria	Cyprus	Armenia	Afghanistan	Cambodia
Burundi	Egypt	Iran	Azerbaijan	Bangladesh	China
Central African Republic	Libya	Iraq	Georgia	India	East Timor
Chad	Morocco	Israel	Tajikistan	Nepal	Indonesia
Congo (Brazzaville)		Jordan	Uzbekistan	Pakistan	Lao
Congo Dem. Rep.		Kuwait		Sri Lanka	Myanmar
Coted'lvoire		Lebanon			North Korea
Djibouti		Syria			South Korea
Eritrea		Turkey			Vietnam
Ethiopia		Yemen			
Ghana					
Guinea					
Guinea Bissau					
Liberia					
Mozambique					
Namibia					
Rwanda					
Senegal					
Sierra Leone					
Somalia					
South Africa					
Sudan					
Togo					
Uganda					
Zimbabwe					

Table Note: tables Part I and II show countries that have been at war, either interstate or civil; does not include civil unrest/protests that resulted in deaths, or disappearance-presumed-dead actions by security forces (political disappearances). Most wars included here ended in late 1980s, 1990s, or 2000s; major wars such as Korean War of the 1950s, and the Vietnam War of the 1960s-1970s have also been included because of the large number of deaths. Source: Smith (2003); Bereovitch and Fretter (2004).

Table 2.9. War Widows Countries—Part II

Pacific Islands	Anglo-Pacific Islands	North America	Caribbean	Central America	South America	Europe incl. Russia
Papua New Guinea	Australia	Canada	Cuba	El Salvador	Argentina	Albania
	New Zealand	USA	Haiti	Guatemala	Peru	Belgium
				Nicaragua		Bosnia
						Croatia
						France
						Germany
						Italy
						Kosovo
						Macedonia
						Montenegro
						Moldova
						Netherlands
						Russia
						Serbia
						Slovenia
						Spain
						UK

Table Note: See note with Part I.

ANNEXURE VI

Genocide Deaths

Genocide, the systematic and large-scale killing of non-combatants, is facilitated by war, and is sometimes the primary purpose of a war. It is therefore the most serious war-related cause of death for the general population, as once organised and put into action, it is difficult to escape and to stop. It is usually perpetrated in the context of a country-wide internal war. The most recent and well-known example is the 1994 Rwandan genocide, in which an estimated 800,000 to one million people were killed. As many as fifty per cent of married women were estimated to have become widows, the majority of whom were over age 30.

Table 1, also using DHS data, shows the effects of the genocide on the number of widows in Rwanda and the change in those number over time, (ten years after the genocide). Notable about this data is the extent to which the number of widows has been quickly dissipating across all age ranges, to the point that the average for the whole age range 15-49, as a percentage of all women 15-49, has effectively reached its pre-genocide level. The result is probably due to reduced rates of marriage and the generally very high mortality rate in the untry between birth and age 30.[1]

Table 2.11. Pre- and Post-Genocide Rwanda: Widows of Child Bearing Age 15-49, Percentages

Rwanda	Year	15-19	20-24	25-29	30-34	35-39	40-44	45-49	15-49
	2005	0.0	0.02	0.9	3.3	8.0	14.6	17.9	4.3
Post-genocide	2000	0.0	1.1	4.3	10.1	16.2	20.3	26.3	7.7
Pre-genocide	1992	0.0	0.8	2.5	4.2	8.0	11.5	16.8	4.1

Table Note: data is for the percentage of widows from the respective age group of *all* women making up that age group, i.e. this is not percentage of a group of widows out of all widows. Source: Rwanda Demographic and Health Survey (DIIS) 2005, 2000 and 1992. OCR Macro International.

In East Timor, formally a part of Indonesia, 200,000 deaths are reported for the period 1975-99, while in Cambodia, the Khmer Rouge regime killed an estimated 1.7 to 2 million people identified as a threat to communism, out of a total country population of seven million. At least one researcher refers to a higher than normal number of widows in Cambodia.[2]

The actions of the Bosnian Serb army has been characterised by international officials as genocide.

Political disappearances are another source of male conflict mortality and a cause of widowhood, the most well known being Argentina, and in Chile. El Salvador during its civil war from 1979-92, experienced some of the worst political repression of opponents of the regime, resulting in some 7,000 disappeared. Open political repression, as in the ongoing case of Zimbabwe, continues to be a problem around the world.[3]

ENDNOTES

[1] Rwanda Demographic and Health Survey (DHS) 2005, final report, Figure 2.1, chapter 2, "Household Characteristics," p. 12. OCR-Macro International (2006).

[2] Rwanda, East Timor and Cambodia death figures, Rosenberg (2003: 229); Lee (2004: 3) makes conflict widows reference and cites statistics of nearly 11 per cent of women widowed as National Institute of Statistics (1999: xii), Cambodia. Currently, there is political violence in West Papua, Indonesia.

[3] This is quite apart from the clandestine political repression that has accompanied the "War on Terror."

ANNEXURE VII

UXO and Other War Deaths

A less well publicised but equally important cause of death for men, with serious economic implications for rural women,[1] is post-conflict, as a result of landmines and unexploded munitions (UXO), ranging from hand grenades to cluster munitions. After landmines, the most insidious UXO is the mortar shell: mortars are called "poor man's artillery" because they are compact weapons. They can be found in regular use in armies across developing countries. Rural people are the main casualties from UXO, because rural people are typically farmers, and therefore disturb landmines and other UXO, leading often to death.

The key aspect of the landmines and UXO problem is its longevity, because clearance is slow and expensive. Therefore they typically remain active for many decades. This is due primarily to the need to destroy them where they lie, because, post-Second World War, landmines were fitted with anti-tamper devices, which makes traditional dig-and-remove clearance impossible.

There are 33 countries, "where landmines constitute a major problem for the civilian population; the situation in five of those countries—Afghanistan, Angola, Cambodia, Iraq and Laos—must be categorised as

Figure 2.4.[4] Global War Deaths, 2000

Estimated Conflict Deaths by Age and Sex, Year 2000

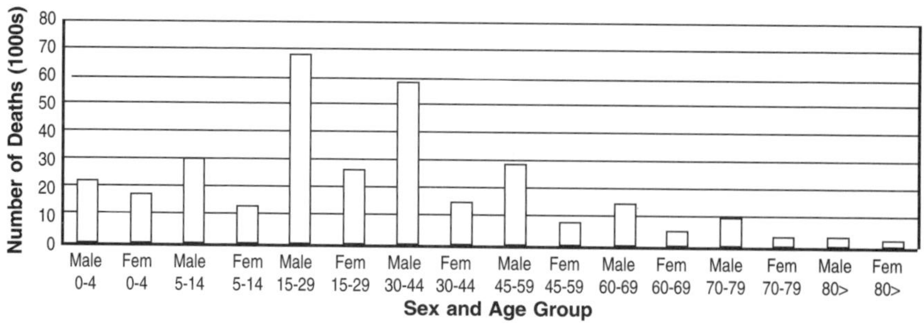

Chart Note: Data source, Murray et al (2002).

an emergency on the basis of the scale of existing [post-war] casualties."[2] It is currently estimated that around 100 million landmines are in the ground around the world.[3]

In terms of the actual number of war widows, no up to date global figure exists, but some better documented country-level examples stand out, although these are country totals, as opposed to actual number of widows produced by the fighting and other war-related hazards. These are Afghanistan with 2 million, Democratic Republic of Congo, 1.9 million, Iraq 740,000 to 1 million, Cambodia, 400,000 and Rwanda, 370,000, Palestine, 96,000 (Loomba Foundation Widows Research Report, 2009).

ENDNOTES

[1] Black (2005:212).

[2] The Mines Advisory Group (MAO) data, quoted in McGrath (1994: I).

[3] Black (2005/212).

[4] This chart was originally presented using the Murray et al (2002) data in Black (ed.), UNRISD (2005: 213).

ANNEXURE VIII

Plight of Widows in Developed Countries

The plight of widows in developed countries has been all but overlooked in terms of research. In part this is probably due to the divide between the west and the third world, with comparisons always reducing the significance of the western findings.

However, many of the indignities suffered by widows in Africa and Asia are also shared by their western counterparts—although obviously to a lesser degree. Poverty exists, rape exists, social exclusion exists, the stigma of widowhood exists—but not to the same extremes as found among widows in Africa and South Asia. As such, it is at most times below the radar of governments and even the media. Whereas these issues do not stand comparison with the deprivations of the third world, they remain very real to those who have to endure them.

What evidence there is of widows' deprivation that exists in the developed countries appears to be concentrated on the older, especially the elderly age groups of women, with the focus mainly on the psychological aspects—bereavement in widowhood. Recent research work on widowhood in the UK reveals this tendency.[1]

However, whether young or old, widows from low-skill, low income backgrounds in the west are still at risk of significant changes for the worse in their standard of living through loss of their husbands' income.

The United States is of particular interest to any study of widows' deprivation in developed countries due to its higher than average incidence of a range of deprivations, from infant mortality to functional illiteracy.[2] "For the past 30 or more years, the poverty rate for elderly widows has persistently been three to four times higher than that for elderly married women. Although policy-makers have repeatedly expressed concern about these high rates, successful policy prescriptions have yet to be adopted."[3]

In particular it was noted, with respect to the United States, that poverty of elderly widows is linked to "the potential for couples to spend substantial portions of their resources on the health care of a sick or dying spouse, leaving the surviving spouse in a precarious financial situation."[4]

This is in no small part due to the severe limitations of the health care system, not in terms of quality of care, but in terms of who can obtain health insurance to avoid otherwise catastrophic medical costs. ...

Health care looms large as a core determinant of human development and so is an ongoing cause of concern for people in poorer countries, or those, such as in Russia, which has experienced a sharp fall in government health expenditure and elimination of at least some free services.

A 2002 World Bank poverty study found that Bosnians considered lack of health care insurance as a key characteristic of poverty. It is instructive, therefore, in the assessment of widows' well-being in the United States, that its healthcare system draws parallels with recovering post-war countries such as Bosnia. US researchers point out that "healthcare ranked first among the issues Americans believe the government should address, and third among the most critical issues facing the country today."[5]

A high poverty rate for US widows has also been observed in a number of other studies.[6] Drawing a parallel with some developing countries, there is evidence of trends, although at smaller orders of magnitude, of widowed grandmothers taking on the primary care role for children after parents have died of HIV/AIDS.[7]

One significant group of widows known to be at risk of deep poverty in the United States are African Americans. The development economist Amartya Sen again singles out the particular plight of African Americans in the US:

"...[with respect to income] African Americans are decidedly poorer than American whites. This is very often seen as an example of relative deprivation of African Americans within the nation, but not compared with poorer people in the rest of the world. Indeed, in comparison with the population of third world countries, African Americans may well be a great many times richer in terms of income, even after taking note of price differences. Seen this way, the deprivation of the American blacks seems to pale to insignificance in the international perspective.

"But is income the right space [metric] in which to make such comparisons? What about the basic capability to live to a mature age, without succumbing to premature mortality? In terms of that criterion the African American men fall well behind the immensely poorer men of China, or the Indian state of Kerala, and also of Sri Lanka, Costa Rica, Jamaica and many other poor economies. [American] black women too fall not only behind white women in the United States but also behind Indian women in Kerala, and come very close to falling behind Chinese women as well. American black men continue to lose ground vis-à-vis the Chinese and Indians over the years—well past the younger ages when death from violence is common."[8]

ENDNOTES

[1] The recent volume is Chambers (2005). See also Bennett (1997) for UK widows psychiatric study.

[2] OECD (2000), (2005).

[3] McGarry and Schoeni (2005: 58).

[4] McGarry and Schoeni (2005: 58).

[5] For Bosnia, Djipa et al (2002: 8); for US health care coverage issues and public opinion surveys reporting health as a major concern, see Mullahy et al (2000).

[6] Hurd and Wise (1989); Hurd (1991); Weir (1998).

[7] Draimin et al (2005).

[8] Sen (1999: 96).

ANNEXURE IX

Children Worst Affected

Table 2.4. Widows' Children Ages 0-4 and 0-17 and Under Five Mortality

Region, Percent of age group	0-4 Total	0-17 Total	U5MWC
North Africa	623,324	1,905,435	44,569
Middle East	655,943	2,399,424	39,090
Sub-Saharan Africa (all countries)	4,104,604	11,625,444	625,033
Sub-Saharan Africa AIDS crisis countries	1,778,229	3,752,358	220,978
Sub-Saharan Africa non-AIDS crisis	2,326,375	7,818,568	404,055
Central Asia	194,902	60,354	10,473
South Asia	5,853,752	21,875,800	557,623
East Asia and Pacific	2,160,748	8,639,448	85,093
South East Asia	1,325,818	4,795,917	59,571
North East Asia	830,184	3,341,022	25,311
Advanced East Asia	132,616	484,388	1,106
Pacific Islands	4,746	17,436	212
Anglo Pacific Islands	11,529	43,269	69
Caribbean	48,413	183,557	2,863
North America	296,321	1,073,685	2,349
Central America	815,470	3,166,077	24,442
South America	2,829,629	10,673,573	109,214
Europe (all) incl. Russia	682,798	2,591,793	9,874
West Europe	196,689	732,744	1,025
Scandinavia (Europe)	7,630	28,916	36
Eastern Europe incl. Russia	486,109	1,859,048	8,849
OECD High Income countries	574,303	2,409,607	3,799
Least Developed Countries	4,044,608	12,129,420	579,365
World Total	18,474,980	64,933,099	1,536,917

Table Note: U5MWC = Under 5 Child Mortality for Widows' Children, actual number of deaths. "Total" of 1,536,917 is the world total, but is not the sum of all column values listed, e.g. sub-Saharan Africa has data compiled for different country groupings. The most recent UNICEF global under five child mortality estimate (for year 2008, released in Sept. 2009) for all children is 8.8 million deaths. Data source, Loomba Foundation (2009) estimates, UN Population Division and individual countries' demographic data. Data denominations are as shown, starting from tens, up to tens of millions.

ANNEXURE X

Key Widows' Issues—a Summary

The following outcomes of becoming a widow are present to differing degrees and combinations in a range of societies around the world:[1]

1. **Property theft and denial of inheritance:** widows arc often forcibly evicted from their homes and extended families by those same family members after the husbands' death, often in what is in effect property theft, in terms of land and building inheritance (assuming the formal and/or customary law allows them to inherit), down even to mundane items such as pots and pans and bedding; the widows are left destitute as homeless "street people";
2. **Superstition and/or cruel beliefs:** due to high levels of superstition in many segments of society in many developing countries, widows are erroneously accused by mothers-in-law and others of having caused the deaths of their husbands, and as a result are subjected to psychological and physical abuse as well as eviction as mentioned in the previous point above;
3. **Discrimination against women:** worst for widows: with particular relevance to widows, deprivation is socially institutionalized when women, regardless of marital status, on those occasions when they can find paid employment, are forced to accept lower wages than men, issues such as illiteracy exacerbating this inequality;
4. **Right to family denied:** under international law, countries are required to "facilitate the family", however, widows' children are sometimes forcibly removed from the widow on the death of the husband; widows' eviction, cited in point (1) above, is also part of denial of right to family;
5. **Child labour:** widows' children from low income families, when not forcibly removed by extended family, often have to enter the labour force as child labourers (defined as children under the age of 15 in most cases with respect to ILO conventions),[2] in order to support their mother and siblings, resulting in lost education and high risk of harm to physical health through hazardous employment, and additional heightened risks associated with children's employment such as physical and sexual abuse;

6. **Widows' re-marriage:** in some cases it is difficult or impossible for widows to remarry, or they may be able to remarry but under unfavourable circumstances, such as, for example, when child and very young adult widows can only find older men to marry, sometimes with older wives still in the household; in other cases widows are forcibly remarried to a dead husband's brother (a traditional customary practice), are often forcibly remarried to a husband's brother, often irrespective of HIV/AIDs having been the cause of death of the husband, or with concern to the HIV/AIDs status of the husband's brother; Hepatitis B and C are another common disease category in developing countries; in other cases they are not permitted to remarry;
7. **Widowhood customs:** widows suffer psychological and physical abuse through traditional post-husband's post-death ritual cleansing ceremonies and rules that can include extended periods of seclusion from normal life that often interferes with paid employment, and/or are socially excluded due to superstition that regards widows as "bad omens", together with having to dress in specific ways, as well as often being barred from remarrying, or not being desired by men for marriage for the preceding reasons;
8. **Child marriage:** child marriage puts girls at a particular disadvantages from many of the above-mentioned issues, with the addition of the reported risk of being used as a sex save by currently married older men whose older wives are no longer sexually desired by them, with the concomitant factor that the older man's children and first wife may retaliate against the effectively captive girl-wife; in addition, child marriage has been used as a cover for, and has resulting in encouraging, human trafficking;
9. **Extreme poverty:** in northern areas of South Asia, widowed women in their forties and fifties have significantly higher mortality than married women in the same age group;
10. **Limited social protection:** in some developed countries, such as the United States and in parts of Eastern Europe, as in most developing countries, the loss of a husband can mean a substantial risk to the continued maintaining of physical health through the loss of occupational/employer health insurance associated with the husbands' employment, as well as the associated loss of income, including pension size reductions;
11. **Discase and public health:** due to traditional customary practice, widows are often forcibly remarried to a husband's brother, often irrespective of HIV/AIDs having been the cause of death of the husband and hence making it likely that the wife is also infected, or with concern to the HIV/AIDs status of the husband's brother

in the case where the widow is not infected; Hepatitis B and C are another very common disease category in developing countries that receives less attention but can be contracted through sexual activity; also, due to the high HIV/AIDS infection rates in many African countries, stigma with respect to fear of HIV/AIDS has developed that now is applied to all widows.

ENDNOTES

[1] This section is based on a range of sources: 1) "Widowhood: invisible women, secluded or excluded", year Dec. 2001 edition of *Women 2000,* published to promote the goals of the Beijing Declaration and the Platform for Action, United Nations Division for the Advancement of Women, Department of Economic and Social Affairs; 2) Margaret Owen (1996) *A World of Women;* 3) Kate Young (2006) "Widows Without Rights: challenging marginalisation and dispossession", *Gender and Development,* Vol. 14, No. 2, July; 4) Betty Potash (ed), (1986) *Widows in African Societies: Choices and Constraints;* 5) Helena Z. Lopata (ed), (1987) *Widows: Volume I, The Middle East, Asia and the Pacific;* 6) Apollo Rwomire (ed), (2001) *African Women and Children: Crisis and Response:* 7) Martha Chen and Jean Dreze (1995) "Widowhood and Well-being in Rural North India", in Monica Das Gupta et al (eds) *Women's Health in India.*

[2] The ILO's 2004 estimate of global child labour, all categories, for age group 5-14 years is 165.8 million out of a total global child population for ages 5-14 in 2004 of 1.206 billion; (corresponding child labour percentage of this total child population cohort is 13.7). Note that an "economically active" child does not always mean a child in child labour: a general formulation definition of child labour is any form of work that is detrimental to the physical and ethical development of the child and that denies them an effective education. This definition is in the spirit of the ILO definition, while the latter employs certain exceptions to the category of "work" with respect to child labour. Above estimates are from *The End of Child Labour: Within Reach,* International Labour Office, Geneva, 2006, p. 6. Available online.

Note: The Annexures are extracts from "Widows Research Report", sponsored by Loomba Foundation. Researcher: Risto F. Harma.

REFERENCES

Ampofo, A.A. 1993. "Controlling and Punishing Women: Violence Against Ghanaian Women," *Review of African Political Economy*. No. 56, March.

Asiimwe, Jacqueline. 2002. "Women and the Struggle for Land in Uganda," chapter 9 in A.M. Tripp and J.C. Kwesiga, *The Women's Movement in Uganda: History, Challenges, and Prospects.* Kampala: Fountain Publishers.

Baden, Sally, Cathy green, Naana Otoo-Oyortey and Tessa Peasgood. 1994. *Background paper on gender issues in Ghana.* Report prepared for West and North Africa Department, Department for International Development (DFID), UK. Bridge Development-Gender, Report No. 19, Institute of Development Studies (IDS), Brighton, UK. http://www.bridge.ids.ac.uk//bridge/Reports/re19c.pdf

Barry, Kathleen. 1996. "Industrialization and Economic Development: The Costs to Women," chapter 9 in Kathleen Barry (ed.) *Vietnam's Women in Transition*. London: Macmillan Press.

Bennett, Kate Mary. 1997. "A Longitudinal Study of Well-being in Widowed Women," *International Journal of Geriatric Psychiatry*. Vol. 12, pp. 61-66.

Bercovitch, Jacob and Judith Fretter 2004. *Regional Guide to International Conflict and Management, 1995-2003.* CQ Press.

Black, Maggie 2005. *Gender and Equality: Striving for Justice in an Unequal World.* Geneva: United Nations Research Institute for Social Development (UNRISD).

Bortei-Dorku, E. 1990. *Profile of Women in Ghana*. Accra: CIDA.

Cambodia Census 1998. National Institute of Statistics, Cambodia. 1999. *General Population Census of Cambodia 1998: Final Census Results*. Phnom Penh, Cambodia: Ministry of Planning.

Carroll, Sherman, Director of Public Affairs, Medical Foundation, Kosovo Field Diary.

Castellino, Joshua, Prof. of Law, Middlesex University, UK, address to a meeting on forced marriage in the UK, organised by Oxfam GB and South Asia Forum UK. Houses of Parliament, 17 June 2009.

Chambers, Pat. 2005. *Older Widows and the Life Course: Multiple Narratives of Hidden Lives*, Aldershot, England: Ashgate Publishing Ltd.

Chang, Leslie T. 2008. *Factory Girls: Voices from the Heart of Modern China*. London: Picador.

Channel Four, UK. 2009. "Nepal: the Living Dead." *Unreported World*. Episode 18, documentary film.

Chant, Sylvia. 2007. *Gender, Generation and Poverty: Exploring the 'Feminisation of Poverty' in Africa, Asia and Latin America*. Cheltenham: Edward Elgar.

Chen, Martha and Jean Drèze. 1995. "Widowhood and Well-Being in Rural North India," chapter 20 in Vandana Madan (ed.) 2002. *The Village in India*. New Delhi: Oxford University Press, excerpted from original published as chapter 9 in Monica Das Gupta and Lincoln C. Chen (eds.), *Women's Health in India: Risk and Vulnerability*. New Delhi: Oxford University Press.

Chen, Martha and Jean Dreze. 1995. "Recent research on widows in India", *Economic and Political Weekly*, No. 30, Sept., pp. 2347-2348

Chen, Martha, Jennifer Sebstad and Lesley O'Connell. 1999. "Counting the Invisible Workforce: The Case of Homebased Workers," *World Development*. No. 27, pp. 603-610.

Department for International Development (DIFD), UK. 2000. *Poverty Elimination and the Empowerment of Women: Strategies for achieving the international development targets*. London: DFID.

Djipa, Dino Mirsada Muzur, and Paula Franklin Lyte. 2002. "Bosnia and Herzegovina: War-Torn Lives", chapter 8 in Deepa Narayan and Patti Petesch (eds.), *Voices of the Poor: From Many Lands*. New York: Oxford University Press and Washington, D.C.: The World Bank.

Draimin, Barbara H. and Warren A. Reich. 2005. "Troubled Tapestries: Children, families, and the HIV/AIDS Epidemic in the United States," chapter 8 in Geoff Foster, Carol Levine and John Williamson (eds.), *A Generation at Risk: The Global Impact of HIV/AIDS on Orphans and Vulnerable Children*. Cambridge: Cambridge University Press.

Feldman, Susan, Julie Byles, Gita Mishra and Jenny Powers. 2002. "The Health and Social Needs of Recently Widowed Older Women in Australia," *Australian Journal of Ageing*. Vol. 21, No. 3, Sept., pp. 135-140.

Guild of Service. 2009. Annual Report 2008-09. New Delhi, India. http://www.guildofservice.org/2008-2009.pdf

Hamalainen, Paivi, Kaija Leena Saarela and Jukka Takala. 2009. "Global trend according to estimated number of occupational accidents and fatal work-related diseases at region and country level," *Journal of Safety Research*, Vol. 40, pp. 125-139.

Harma, Risto F. 2008. Widowed Bangladeshi Garment Worker, "Salma's"

Account of the Working Conditions in the Bangladesh Export Garment Industty Factories, 2008. Notes from group interview, London.

Hasan, Masuma. 2006. Overview report on widows in Pakistan submitted to the Loomba Foundation for Loomba Foundation International Widows Day 2006.

Home Office, UK (2004). *Report of the Fact Finding Mission to India, Women in India*, 11-24 July 2004, Country Information and Policy Unit, Immigration and Nationality Directorate, Home Office, UK. http://rds.homeoffice.gov.uk/rds/pdfs06/india_ffm0704_250106.doc

Horrell, Sara and Pramila Krishnan. 2007. "Poverty and Productivity in Female-Headed Households in Zimbabwe." *Journal of Development Studies*. Vol. 43, No. 8, pp 1351-1380.

Human Rights Watch (HRW) 2003. Interview with Kenyan widow Susan Wagitangu, Nairobi, October 29, 2002 and Kenyan widow Emily Owino, November 2, 2002, in *Double Standards*. http://www.hrw.org/en/node/12352/section/1 Accessed August 2009.

Hurd, Michael D. 1991. "Changing Social Security Survivorship Benefits and the Poverty of Widows," *National Bureau of Economic Research* (NBER) Working Paper.

Hurd, Michael D., and David A. Wise. 1989. "The Wealth and Poverty of Widows: Assets before and after the Husband's Death," in David A. Wise (ed.), *Economics of Aging*. Chicago: University of Chicago Press.

International Labour Organization (ILO). 2006. *The End of Child Labour: Within Reach*, International Labour Office, Geneva,

— — 2004, 28 April. "28 April, World Day for Safety and Health at Work—Two million work deaths a year: A preventable tragedy," http://www.ilo.org/global/About_the_ILO/Media_and_public_information/Feature_stories/lang—en/WCMS_075605/index.htm Accessed July 2009.

J.M., Atinga Kwame. 2004. "A Case Study on HIV/AIDS prevalence trends in Kisumu district in Kenya: the example of the Luo community's cultural inflictions and afflictions." Fifteenth International Conference on AIDS, July 2004, Bangkok, Thailand.

Jayatunge, Ruwan M. 2010. "The Mental Health Issues of Sri Lankan War Widows," *The Sunday Leader*, Sri Lanka, 28 March. http://www.thesundayleader.lk/2010/03/28/the-mental-health-issues-of-sri-lankan-war-widows/

Kidon Felomon interview, March 2004, by Worku Zerai for FAO Sub-Regional Office for Southern and East Africa, reproduced in Izumi, Kaori (ed.). 2006. *Reclaiming Our Lives: HIV and AIDS, Women's Land and Property Rights and Livelihoods in Southern and East Africa, Narrative and Responses*. Cape Town: Human Sciences Research Council (HSRC).

Lee, Susan H. 2005. "The Long-Term Effects of War on Rural Cambodian

Widows," Paper presented at the annual meeting of the American Sociological Association, Marriott Hotel, Loews Philadelphia Hotel, Philadelphia, PA, Aug. 12, 2005.

— — 2004. "'Rice Plus' and Family Solidarity: Rural Cambodian Widows' Economic Coping Practices." *Paper presented at the annual meeting of the American Sociological Association, Hilton San Francisco & Renaissance Park 55 Hotel, San Francisco, CA,*, Aug 14, 2004. http://www.allacademic.com/meta/p109329_index.html Accessed Aug. 2009.

Loomba Foundation. 2009. *Widows Research Report 2010: The Global Overview of Deprivation Faced by Women as Widows*. New York: Loomba Foundation.

Lopata, Helena Z. 1973. *Widowhood in an American City*. Piscataway, NJ: Transaction Publishers.

— — (ed), (1987) *Widows: Volume 1, The Middle East, Asia and the Pacific.* Durham, NC: Duke University Press.

Lopez, Alan D., Colin D. Mathers, Majid Ezzati, Dean T. Jamison and Christopher J. L. Murray (eds.). 2006. *Global Burden of Disease and Risk Factors*. New York and Washington, D. C.: Oxford University Press and The World Bank.

Magoke-Mhoja, Monica Elias 2008. *Child-Widows Silenced and Unheard: Human Rights Sufferers in Tanzania.* Milton Keynes: Author House.

Marsden, Peter. 1998. *The Taliban: War, Religion and the New Order in Afghanistan.* London: Zed Books.

McGarry, Kathleen and Robert F. Schoeni. 2005, "Medicare Gaps and Widow Poverty," *Social Security Bulletin*, Vol. 66, No. 1, pp. 58-74.

McGrath, Rae 1994. *Landmines: Legacy of Conflict – A Manual for Development Workers*. Oxford: Oxfam GB.

Medecins sans Frontieres (MSF). 31 March 2008, "Winners and Losers in India: a major humanitarian crisis in a booming economy", Field News press release. http://www.doctorswithoutborders.org/news/article.cfm?id=2581 (Accessed April 2009).

Mehta, Ajay. 2000. "The Micro Politics of Participatory Projects: An Anatomy of Change in Two Villages," chapter 2 in Pauline E. Peters (ed.), *Development Encounters: Sites of Participation and Knowledge*. Cambridge. MA: Harvard Institute for International Development, Harvard University.

Moorehead, Caroline. 2003. "Afghanistan: land of widows," *Open Democracy*, London. 22 June. http://www.opendemocracy.net/people/article_1303.jsp

Mpendwa, M. A. 2002. "What has happened/is happening to HIV/AIDS Positive Widows in Tanzania - Africa. Paper presented at the Fourteenth International Conference on AIDS, July 2002, Barcelona, Spain.

Mullahy, John, and Barbara L. Wolfe. 2000. "Health Policies for the Non-Elderly Poor," chapter 8 in Sheldon H. Danziger and Robert H. Havemen (eds.) *Understanding Poverty*. New York: Russell Sage Foundation and Cambridge, MA: Harvard University Press.

Murray, C. J. L., g. King, A. D. Lopez, N. Tomijima and E. G. Krug 2002. "Armed Conflict as a Public Health Problem." *British Medical Journal*, Vol. 324, pp. 346-349.

New Internationalist. 2007. *The World Guide*, 11th edition. Oxford: New Internationalist Publications Ltd.

Nicholas, Peter M. 2000. "Home Video: War Widows Relive Vietnam," *New York Times*, 5 May. http://www.nytimes.com/2000/05/05/movies/home-video-war-widows-relive-vietnam.html

Nordheimer, Jon 1996. "One Day's Death Toll on the Job." *New York Times*, December 22, pp. F1, F10, F11.

Okioma, Mary. 2004. "Brideprice: Paving the Way for a Killer," paper presented at the International Conference on Brideprice and Development, Kampala: Mifumi Project.

One World Action. 2001. *Developing Gender-Sensitive Local Services*, One World Action seminar (London, 28-29 June 2000) Report. London: The British Council.

ORC Macro International, *Rwanda Demographic and Health Survey (DHS) 2005*. Calverton, Maryland, USA.

– – *Rwanda Demographic and Health Survey (DHS) 2000*. Calverton, Maryland, USA.

– – *Rwanda Demographic and Health Survey (DHS) 1992*. Calverton, Maryland, USA.

Organisation for Economic Cooperation and Development (OECD) and Statistics Canada. 2005. *Learning a Living: First Results of the Adult Literacy and Life Skills Survey*. Paris: OECD.

Organisation for Economic Cooperation and Development (OECD) and Statistics Canada. 2000. *Literacy in the Information Age: Final Report of the International Adult Literacy Survey*. Paris: OECD.

Owen, Margaret. 2006. "Out of the Past: Widows in Nepal are traditionally shunned by their communities—but the current unrest is giving them a chance to fight for their rights," *The Guardian*, 24 April. http://www.guardian.co.uk/world/2006/apr/24/gender.nepal

— — 2002. Empowering Widows in Development, Non-Governmental Organisation Report, London, cited in P. Adinarayana Reddy, 2004. *Problems of Widows in India*. New Delhi: Sarup and Sons.

— — 1996. *A World of Widows*. London: Zed Books.

Oxfam International. 2002. *Rigged Rules and Double Standards: Trade, Globalisation, and the Fight Against Poverty*. Oxford: Oxfam International.

Potash, Betty (ed.) 1986. *Widows in African Societies: Choices and Constraints*.

Stanford: Stanford University Press.

Rahman, M. Omar. 1990. "Gender Differences in Marriage and Mortality for the Elderly in Rural Bangladesh", paper submitted as part of PhD thesis to Dept. of Epidemiology, Harvard School of Public Health, Harvard University.

Rai, Shirin M. 2008. *The Gender Politics of Development. London*: Zed Books.

Rosenberg, Jerome 2003. "Megadeaths: Individual Reactions and Social Responses to Massive Loss of Life," in Clifton D. Bryant (ed) *Handbook of Death and Dying*. Thousand Oaks: Sage Publications, Inc.

Rwanda Census 2002. *Synthese des Analyses des Donnees du Recensement – 2002 du Rwanda*. 3ème Recensement General de al Population et de L'Habitat au 15 Aout 2002. Ministere des Finances et de la Planification Economique, Service National de Recensement. Kigali. Février 2005.

Rwomire, Appollo (ed.). 2001. *African Women and Children: Crisis and Response*. Westport, CA: Praeger.

Sangtin Writers and Richa Nagar. 2006. *Playing with Fire: Feminist Thought and Activism through Seven Lives in India*. London: University of Minnesota Press.

Seabrook, Jeremy. 2002. "Ghosts in the city of widows," *New Statesman*, 16 December. http://www.newstatesman.com/200212160029

Sen, Amartya. 1999. *Development as Freedom*. Oxford: Oxford University Press.

Shamim, Ishrat. 1993. *Riverine Hazards, Erosion and Displacement: Coping Mechanisms of Rural Women as Managers of Households*, Winrock International, Dhaka, May, (mimeo).

Shamim, I. and K. Salahuddin. 1992. "Women in urban informal sector: Employment pattern, activity types and problems," *Women for Women*, Vol. 18, pp. 4-5, Dhaka.

Smith, Dan 2003. *The Atlas of War and Peace*. London: Earthscan Publications.

Stillwaggon, Eileen. 2009. Personal correspondence with Loomba Foundation Widows Research Report (2009) author Risto F. Harma.

Stillwaggon, Eileen 1998. *Stunted Lives, Stagnant Economies: Poverty, Disease and Underdevelopment*. Newbrunswick: Rutgers University Press.

Todaro, Michael P. and Stephen C. Smith. 2009. *Economic Development*. 10th edition. London: Addison-Wesley.

Torres, Alissa. 2009. *American Widow*. New York: Villard.

Tribe, Rachel and Padmal De Silva. 1999. "Psychological Intervention with Displaced Widows in Sri Lanka", *International Review of Psychiatry*. Vol. 11, Issues 2 & 3, pp. 184-190. January.

United Nations Economic Commission for Africa (UNECA). 1984. *Law and Status of Women in Ghana*. African Training and Research Centre for Women, Research Series. Addis Ababa, Ethiopia: UNECA.

United Nations Division for the Advancement of Women. 2001.

"Widowhood: invisible women, secluded or excluded", December 2001 issue of *Women 2000*, United Nations Division for the Advancement of Women, Department of Economics and Social Affairs, New York: United Nations. http://www.un.org/womenwatch/daw/public/wom_Dec%2001%20single%20pg.pdf

United Nations Development Fund for Women (UNIFEM). 2006. *Gender Profile of the Conflict in Afghanistan*. Accessed 7 July 2006.

— — 2003. *Not a Minute More: Ending Violence Against Women*. New York: UNIFEM.

United Nations Educational, Scientific and Cultural Organization (UNESCO). 2005. *Education for All (EFA) Global Monitoring Report 2006: Literacy for Life*. UNESCO, Paris.

United Nations Food and Agriculture Organisation (FAO). 1995. *Women, Agriculture and Rural Development in the Near East: Findings of an FAO Study*. FAO, Rome.

United Nations Population Division 2009. *World Population Prospects: The 2008 Revision*. Online version: http://www.un.org/esa/population/

Vaux, Tony. 2001. *The Selfish Altruist: Relief Work in Famine and War*. London: Earthscan Publications, Ltd.

Von Struensee, Vanessa. 2005. "Widows, Child Marriage and AIDS", posted by Subidita Chatterjee on "Women and Health", Phase 3, Week 1, Rights and Needs of HIV Positive Women and Women/Girls Vulnerable to HIV, United Nations online E-forum, UN Department of Economic and Social Affairs, 14 Jan. 2005. http://esaconf.un.org/WB/default.asp?action=9&boardid=26&read=1836&fid=317

Von Struensee, Vanessa. 2004. "Widows, AIDS, Health and Human Rights in Africa," London School of Economics Crisis States Research Centre, London. P 68 check ref that this is it JD MPH the most oppressed violated and invisible and their voices are the most unheard millions of widows are young mothers some still children all subject to extreme discriminatory report cited p. 69.

Watt, Jonathan. Monday 24 March 2005. "Blood and Coal: the human cost of cheap Chinese goods." *The Guardian*, London. http://www.guardian.co.uk/world/2005/mar/14/china.jonathanwatts Accessed: July 2009.

Weir, David 1998. "Prospects for Widow Poverty," Pension Research Council, Working Paper.

Wilson, David and Mariam Claeson. 2009. "Dynamics of the HIV Epidemic in South Asia," chapter 1 in Markus Haacker and Mariam Claeson (eds.) *HIV and AIDS in South Asia: An Econoic Development Risk*. Washington, D. C.: The World Bank.

Women's Centre for Legal Aid and Counselling. 1995. *Towards Equality: An Examination of the Status of Palestinian Women in Existing Law*.

Women's Centre for Legal Aid and Counselling, Jerusalem.

World Bank. 2008a. *World Development Indicators 2008*. Washington, D. C.: The World Bank.

World Bank. 2008b. *Poverty Data: A Supplement to World Development Indicators 2008*. Downloadable only. Washington, D.C.: The World Bank.

World Public Opinion 2008. "Poll: Across the World Many See Discrimination Against Widows and Divorced Women," [Widows Survey].

http://www.worldpublicopinion.org/pipa/articles/btjusticehuman_rightsra/494.php Accessed June 2009.

Young, Kate. 2006. "Widows without rights: challenging marginalisation and dispossession." *Gender & Development*, Vol. 14, No. 2, July, pp. 199-209.

INDEX

International
Widows Day
June 23rd
THE
LOOMBA
TRUST